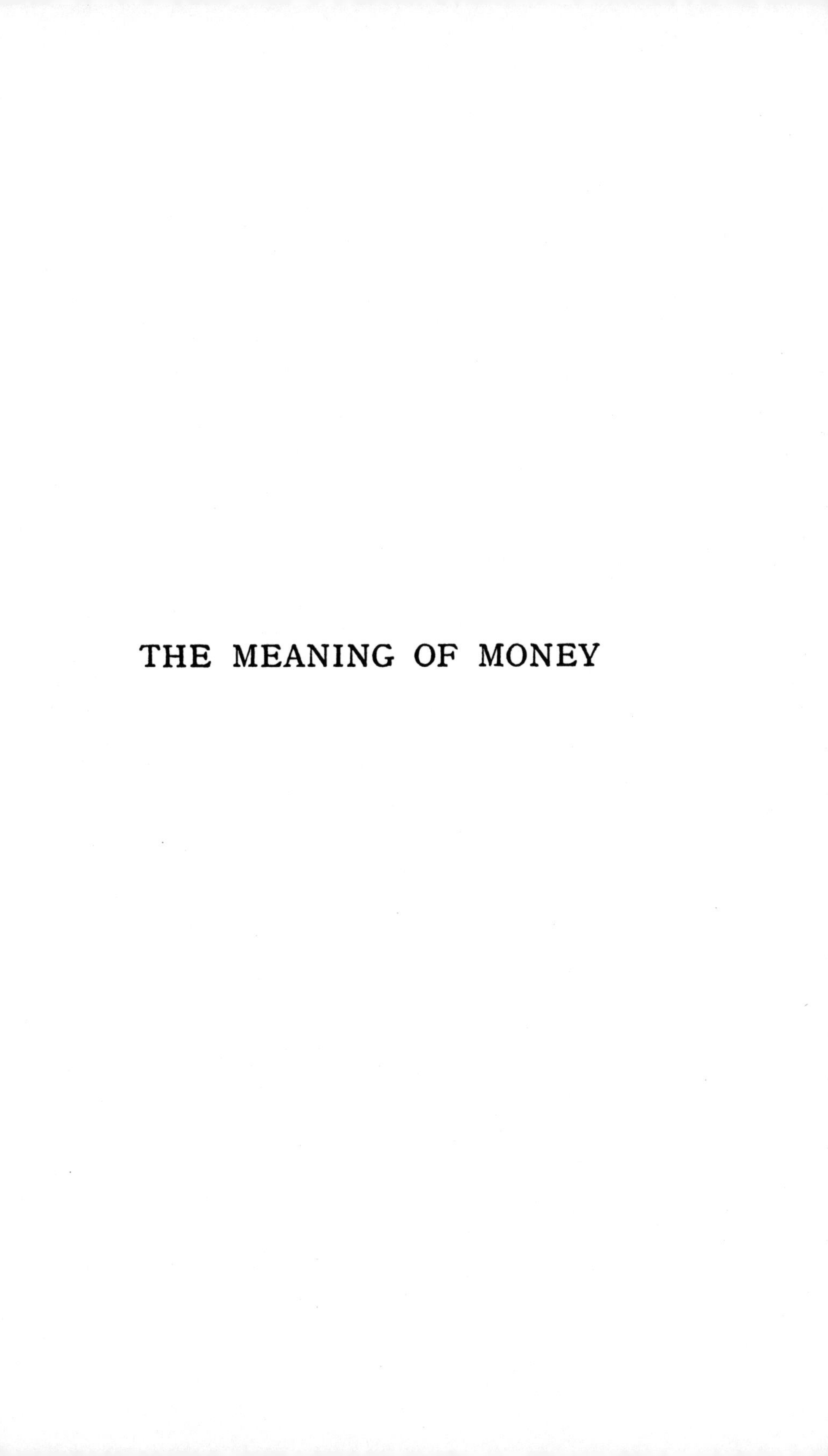

THE MEANING OF MONEY

THE
MEANING OF MONEY

BY

HARTLEY WITHERS

"Grau, theurer Freund, ist alle Theorie
Und grün des Lebens goldner Baum."
GOETHE.

LONDON
SMITH, ELDER & CO., 15, WATERLOO PLACE
1909

PRINTED BY
WILLIAM CLOWES AND SONS, LIMITED
LONDON AND BECCLES

PREFACE

THIS book is designed to meet the difficulty experienced by the average reader in understanding that part of a newspaper City article which deals with the money market. It has been compiled with as little reference as possible to other books, and chiefly expresses views and facts gathered from practical men at work in the great machine which it describes, one of whom has kindly read the proofs and made valuable suggestions. The difficulties of the subject are very real to its writer, who has consequently aimed earnestly at clearness, risking platitude and iteration to achieve it. Its shortcomings will be pardoned, by considerate readers, on the ground of the limited leisure in which it was written.

CONTENTS

CHAPTER IV

THE BILL OF EXCHANGE

CHAPTER V

THE MANUFACTURE OF MONEY

CHAPTER VI

LONDON THE WORLD'S MONETARY CLEARING HOUSE

CHAPTER VII

THE CHEQUE-PAYING BANKS

CHAPTER VIII

THE BILL-BROKERS AND DISCOUNT HOUSES

CHAPTER IX

THE ACCEPTING HOUSES AND FOREIGN BANKS

CHAPTER X

THE FOREIGN EXCHANGES

CHAPTER XI

THE BANK OF ENGLAND

CHAPTER XII

BANK RATE AND MARKET RATE

CHAPTER XIII

THE BANK RETURN

CHAPTER XIV

THE GOLD RESERVE

THE MEANING OF MONEY

CHAPTER I

INTRODUCTORY

THE meaning of Money is not a question of economic theory. The object of this volume is to explain a matter of plain, positive, practical fact, which is very important, very dull and very little understood; and to do so as clearly as may be, and with the least possible use of the alarming apparatus which generally affrights the casual reader who opens a book on a monetary subject. No columns of statistics will be paraded and deployed, the use of diagrams will be sedulously avoided, and as far as possible figures will be ruled out.

The word Money is associated with much confusion and difficulty in the minds of those who have not been obliged to think the matter out, because of the different senses in which it is used. In one sense it is perfectly simple, without the least reflection or examination. Everybody understands money in the sense of the pounds, shillings, and pence that we pay in the shape of coin, notes or cheques for everyday wants. But the other most common use of the word leads to complication, because in its second sense money means not money, but the loan of money.

This is the sense in which the word is used when we speak of a money market or a price of money, phrases which are wholly incomprehensible to those to whom this difference of meaning is not made clear. Any one who defines money roughly as a sovereign in his pocket, with which he can buy whatever he wants up to the extent of its purchasing power, does so quite naturally, for this is its most obvious meaning. But having got this meaning into his head, he is unable, and again quite naturally, to understand strange expressions in the newspapers which tell him that money is cheap or that the money market is tight. He knows that the price of a thing is the number of sovereigns, or fractions of a sovereign, that it will fetch. He also knows that no one will give him more than a sovereign for the sovereign that he has in his pocket, and he is equally convinced that the most cunning sophistries of the most skilful dialectician would never induce him to part with it for less. He therefore proceeds triumphantly to the conclusion that it is nonsense to talk about a price for money, and his argument is perfectly sound on the premises from which he starts.

His mistake arises from the fact that, as has been

stated, money is often used in a quite different sense, namely, the loan of money; or perhaps the matter can be made still clearer if we express it by saying that the words "price" and "market" are applied in a different sense when applied to money from their meaning in connection with any ordinary commodity. The price of a hat is the sovereign that you pay to become its owner; the price of money is the sovereign or sovereigns that you promise to pay some day for the loan or temporary use of it. The market in wool or wheat is the place where you can buy these articles from the assembled merchants or dealers. The money market is the place in which you can borrow money.

It thus becomes apparent that the phrase which has proved a stumblingblock to so many generations of schoolboys and more mature students—that money is a commodity which can be bought and sold like any other—is not true. Money is certainly a commodity, but it cannot be bought and sold like any other, for that would imply exchanging it for itself, since buying and selling are nothing but the exchange of commodities for money, as distinguished from barter, which is exchanging commodities for one another. Money can be borrowed or lent, and this is at once a perfectly reasonable and comprehensible transaction, which would never cause the least bewilderment in the mind of the most unmathematical schoolboy. It is perfectly clear to Jones, minor, that it might be to his advantage, in the lean and hungry days towards the end of term, to take five shillings in hard cash and to promise to pay seven-and-six after the holidays, when everybody's pocket is bursting with metallic evidences of family affection. And this transaction, allowance being made for local and psychological variations, is a fair specimen of the business done every day in Lombard Street and in the other money markets of the world.

The money market, then, is the place in which money down is exchanged for the promise of money some day. And as the borrower, the man who wants money down, must obviously offer the lender an inducement to let him have it, it will always be found that the amount of money promised some day by the borrower is bigger than the amount of money paid down by the lender. The difference between the two figures is the rate of interest, which is often loosely and confusingly described as the price of money.

This rate of interest, as every one knows, is calculated "per cent.," so much on each £100 borrowed. If you borrow £1000 for a year from your banker, and he charges you 3 per cent., or £3 per £100 for the advance, he will give you the right to draw a cheque now for £1000, or to withdraw this amount in coin or notes, and at the end of the year you will owe him £1030. But this simple statement of the matter is complicated slightly in usual practice, because the interest is probably payable periodically at the quarter or half-year. This complication becomes important in the case of loans for long or indefinite periods, but the broad fact remains that the chief operations of the money market consist of giving cash down in return for the promise of a little more cash some day, or of annual or half-yearly cash payments.

Time is thus the distinctive element in the most ordinary and obvious transactions of the money market, and clears away the difficulty which besets those who cannot understand how a money market can exist. To exchange money for money would be absurd; to exchange money now for more money some day is evidently a quite reasonable convenience to a borrower who hopes to make a profitable use of the sum borrowed, and to earn more by its employment than the price that he will have to pay for it. And space is the other element which accounts for the rest of the market's operations. Besides giving and taking money down in return for money some day, it is also engaged in giving and taking money here for money somewhere else. Hence arises the complicated and difficult mechanism of what is generally called "exchange," which also becomes a comparatively simple matter when it is clearly expressed and freed from confusing technicalities. The broad meaning of it is clear enough, if you reflect that when you buy a postal order you are conducting an exchange transaction. You receive a communication from a tradesman in a town in which you formerly lived to the effect that his account, amounting to five shillings, has been long outstanding, and that he would be glad to have it settled. The five shillings are ready enough in your pocket, but the question is, how to get them, for example, from London to Bristol. You can put two half-crowns in an envelope, register it, and so send your money at the cost of threepence. But the cheaper and more convenient method is to pay some one who has money in Bristol something to induce him to pay your debt for you there. That some one is ready in the person of the Post Office, which sells you an order for five shillings, payable at any office in the United Kingdom, for five shillings plus a penny. You put the order in an envelope and send the money at a total cost of twopence, and your tradesman presents it at the Bristol post-office and receives cash. Thus you have carried out an exchange transaction, which may be technically expressed by saying that you have bought a draft on Bristol, and forwarded it to your creditor, and that it has been met on presentation.

Monetary transactions may thus be divided into three main divisions:—

(1) Those in which money is exchanged for any kind of commodity or service; ordinary buying or selling operations.

(2) Those in which money down is exchanged for the promise of money some day; these include all kinds of loan operations, from the discounting of a bill due sixty days hence to an issue of a war loan by the British Government.

(3) Those in which money here is exchanged for money somewhere else; and these are exchange operations, which have been crudely exemplified by the purchase of a postal order, but are by far the most complicated kind of monetary business, including such transactions as turning sovereigns into Shanghai taels, composed of silver, or into inconvertible paper notes, issued by some South American Republic.

It will be observed that in all three there is one constant factor, which is money here and now, or cash. In ordinary buying and selling cash is exchanged for goods or services, as when we buy a pair of gloves across the counter of a shop, or send a reluctant cheque to pay a dentist's account or a lawyer's bill of costs. In loan operations cash is exchanged for some form of security or promise to pay. In exchange operations cash is exchanged for drafts representing a right to money in some other place. And before we can go any further, it will be necessary to give some explanation of the different forms taken by cash, or money here and now. Everybody knows that when a payment is to be made it will take the form of coin, Bank of England notes, or, most probably, a cheque drawn on a banker; and the stages by which these forms of payment came into being are a well-worn story, which must be summarized briefly in the interests of clearness and completeness.

CHAPTER II

COINED CASH

THE most obvious of the forms of cash is the coined currency that we carry in our pockets, consisting of gold, silver, and bronze discs, stamped with the image and superscription of the king, and milled round the edges to prevent enterprising bullionists from shaving metal off their rims. This precaution, it will be observed, is not considered necessary in the case of the penny.

The most potent of these, in extracting goods and services from mankind, is gold. Since the purpose of this volume is an endeavour to make money matters, as they are, clear and comprehensible, there is no need to enter into a historical dissertation on the steps which have raised gold into its position as the most important medium of exchange, legal tender to any amount, and consequently, as we shall see later, the basis of credit, or of the lender's side of credit. (On the borrower's side there must be some sort of security as a basis.) But the more obvious reasons which produced this result may be enumerated. We have already seen that buying is distinguished from barter by being an exchange of goods for money instead of an exchange of goods for goods. The inconvenience of a state of barter is evident on a moment's reflection, and it need not be said that as long as it prevailed commercial progress was almost impossible. The sad state of the hungry hatter, unable, in the days of barter, to get meat because the butcher wants not hats but boots, is a commonplace of the economic text-books, and it is clear at once that a long step forward has been taken when a community agrees to recognize one commodity as always acceptable in payment for others, so that any capitalist who is possessed of a store of it may always rely on being able to convert it into whatever he needs that is produced by his fellows. It is also evident that the commodity selected had to be endowed with certain qualities, chief among which were that it should be lasting, easy to pass from hand to hand, and fairly uniform, that is, with not too great a difference in size and desirability between its various examples. The Old Testament story shows that in the primitive society depicted by it a man's wealth was gauged by the size of his flocks and herds and the number of his changes of raiment, and in the Homeric poems fine suits of armour are valued by the number of kine that they would fetch. Other instances of the use of articles of common consumption as currency include tobacco, hides, shells, bullets and nails. But the prevalence of beasts was sufficient to lead etymologists to consider at one time that the Latin word for a beast, *pecus*, had been enshrined in the name for money, *pecunia*, which has come down in English in its negative form, impecunious. This derivation is now abandoned, comparative philology having decided that *pecunia* is the same word as the English "fee," and is chiefly memorable for having prompted a passage, full of vivid fancy and inspiration, in Carlyle's "Sartor Resartus." "A simple invention it was," says Herr Teufelsdröckh, "in the old-world Grazier—sick of lugging his slow Ox about the country till he got it bartered for corn or oil—to take a piece of Leather, and thereon scratch or stamp the mere Figure of an Ox (or *Pecus*); put it in his pocket, and call it *Pecunia*, Money. Yet hereby did Barter grow Sale, the Leather Money is now Golden and Paper, and all miracles have been out-miracled: for there are Rothschilds and English National Debts; and whoso has sixpence is sovereign (to the length of sixpence) over all men; commands Cooks to feed him, Philosophers to teach him, Kings to mount guard over him—to the length of sixpence."

The ox was certainly at one time a standard of value, though it may be doubted whether it passed generally as currency, even stamped on leather, for Carlyle's hypothesis really requires a rather advanced stage of credit organization, with token money issued by graziers, and apparently accepted by a trusting and economically civilized public. But in any case the ox must have been singularly ill-adapted for currency purposes; not only was it not lasting, but it was certain to deteriorate after a certain age, and finally to perish; it was very far from portable, as Carlyle's Grazier found; and the difference between one ox and another in size, value, and other respects is so great that the kine circulation must have been singularly liable to the action of the great economic principle known as Gresham's Law, under which, as we shall see later, bad currency drives out good.

All this has been somewhat laboriously set forth, because in these respects the ox is the very antithesis of the gold-piece, and having seen wherein the ox failed, we have already grasped the advantages of the sovereign.

The sovereign is permanent;* portable, and of universal acceptability, either in its own shape or melted back into its original bullion. As it emerges from the Mint, there is no appreciable difference between it and its fellows, and its long use as the standard money of the leading commercial nation

* Comparatively permanent, that is. It is not wholly impervious to wear and tear, and M. de Launay, in his work on "The World's Gold," estimates that a gold coin would entirely disappear in eight thousand years.

has given it a position which is unrivalled in the present and unparallelled in the past. The different experiences to which one sovereign and another may be subjected make a difference to the length of time during which they preserve their full weight, but weight rarely becomes a question of practical importance to holders of the sovereign considered as cash, though it occasionally does so to bullion dealers, who regard the sovereign merely as a piece of gold that may be melted into bars. The coinage is now so well cared for that for purposes of inland and retail exchange one may be taken to be as good as another, as long as we are certain that it is a real sovereign, duly stamped and milled. We are apt to take this inestimable convenience as a matter of course, but it is only secured by constant vigilance on the part of the responsible authorities, and throughout the Middle Ages untold loss, inconvenience and uncertainty was caused by the chronically chaotic state of the currency in this and other countries.

In those good old days, monarchs who did not actually debase their own currencies by decreasing the amount of true metal in them, and then passing them to their unsuspecting subjects, were regarded as enlightened and disinterested reformers; and the imperfect methods of coinage employed even by the best-intentioned made it easy to sweat and clip the coins, that is to say, to shave bits off them and then pass them on. Here came in the opportunity of the bullion dealer, and the process arose which went on undetected for centuries until it was enounced and denounced by Sir Thomas Gresham, Queen Elizabeth's great monetary adviser, who stated his famous economic law on the subject. The gist of which is, that if two coins are in circulation, one better than the other, the good one will be held back by any one who is wise enough to recognize its merits, and the bad one will be passed on; so that after a time only the clipped and sweated coins will be circulating in the hands of the public, and the full-weighted ones will be either in the vaults of the bullion dealers or melted into bars. To protect themselves against the working of this law, our forefathers used sometimes to carry a small pair of scales, with weights representing a guinea and a half-guinea, fitted into a neat case to be tucked into the pocket.

It has been claimed for gold, that one of its great advantages, which helped to raise it to its position of predominance as circulating medium and basis of credit, is its steadiness in value. It is, in fact, a common delusion that the value of gold is fixed and never varies. The value of gold appears to be fixed by the law which compels the Mint to take any gold that is brought to it and coin it into sovereigns at the rate of £3 17*s.* 10½*d.* per oz., but that is only another way of expressing the fact that a coined sovereign is equivalent to so much gold; but because we are accustomed to value everything in sovereigns many of us have been led into the assumption that gold which can always be made into so many sovereigns per oz. must therefore be unchangeable in value. But if we keep fast hold of the fact that the value of a thing is what it will fetch, it will be seen at once that the sovereign, or the gold from which it is coined, has no such charmed prerogative. When wheat is 35*s.* a quarter the buying power of the sovereign, in the pocket of the miller who wants to buy wheat, is different from its value when wheat is 25*s.* But though the value of gold can be no more fixed than that of anything else, at the same time its comparative indestructibility, and the enormous amount of it in existence in one shape or another, make its value depend much less than that of most other things on the amount of the output at the moment.

Wheat, which is grown to be consumed straightway, depends for its price on the prospects of the present crop and the amount left over of the last; gold, which is mined in order to be kept in the form of plate, ornaments, coins and ingots, and is only consumed by dentists, is obviously much less dependent on the chances which may be tending to increase its amount more or less rapidly than usual. For whatever its form, it may always be brought out and melted, and so come into the market in the shape of cash, as was recognized by the prudent Athenians* when in the days of their prosperity they overlaid the statue of Athene with gold, giving it a gorgeous appearance for the time being and leaving a reserve which could at any time be stripped off and turned into the sinews of war. Gold thus may be regarded as less likely to fluctuate in value than most other commodities owing to the huge accumulated supply, which renders the new output for the time being a matter of comparatively little importance; and this fact, which has sometimes been exaggerated into a statement that its value is fixed, has certainly contributed, with its beauty as decoration and its commanding merits as currency, to the universal acceptability of gold, in economically civilized countries, in payment for goods and services.

It is doubtless a mere convention that gives gold its commanding position, and it may be contended that it would be much simpler, cheaper and more civilized to conduct exchanges by means of pieces of paper secured on national property, as the French Revolutionists tried to do with their *assignats*, or to abolish all need for mediums of exchange and help ourselves to whatever we want, rendering honest service in exchange by the mere impulse of our own consciences. But we are not concerned at present with any theoretical questions

* Thucydides, ii. 13.

of an ideal currency or absence of currency. The only currency that is of practical and everyday importance is that which is endowed with the virtue of universal acceptability. If the trading community will take a certain piece of metal everywhere in payment for its goods and services, that piece of metal is good currency; and no most scientifically evolved substitute will take its place until it has won its way to the possession of the same virtue. And the fact cannot be gainsaid that gold is the one commodity which is universally and at all times acceptable in all civilized communities, and that all forms of promise to pay, or paper money, are acceptable in proportion to the readiness with which they can be turned into gold. And consequently we shall find, when we come to deal with the more interesting problems of the manufacture of credit, that the convertibility of credit into gold is a matter that its manufacturers always have to consider and allow for carefully, and that consequently the amount of gold that they may possess in order to meet credit instruments that come in for conversion, is necessarily a very important factor among those which regulate the amount of credit that they can, or ought to, create.

But even when the importance of gold as the universally acceptable medium of exchange is admitted, it is often denied, by economic theorists and other critically-minded observers, that the amount of available gold is a question of any moment. In theory it is easy to argue that, if the amount of gold were suddenly doubled, the world at large would not be a penny the richer, because the buying power of the gold would be halved, the price of everything would be doubled, we should have twice as many sovereigns in our pockets, and should have to pay twice as much for everything that we wanted. But I venture to think that it is easy even in theory to push this contention too far; because any such great addition to currency and credit would have a great effect in stimulating production, and so would lead to a great addition to the number of real goods which humanity desires and consumes when it can get them. In so far as this was so, the condition of humanity as a whole would be materially improved. Trade would be more active, and the many borrowers who are almost always in search of credit for the promotion of various productive enterprises would be more easily provided. In fact, the extent to which trade and economic progress have in the past been quickened by additions to the supply of the precious metals has produced a theory, with respectable authority behind it, which connects the development of civilization with mining activity. Perhaps the most stalwart and uncompromising exposition of this theory is given by Sir Archibald Alison in his "History of Europe." "The two greatest events,"* he says, "which have occurred in the history of mankind have been directly brought about by a successive contraction and expansion of the circulating medium of society." These events were the fall of the Roman Empire, which, according to Sir Archibald, "was in reality brought about by a decline in the gold and silver mines of Spain and Greece," and the Renaissance, which he ascribes to the discovery of the mines of Mexico and Peru.

Between these two theoretical extremes—one maintaining that the available volume of the precious metals is a matter of no importance, the other regarding it as the cause of the most momentous events in human development—it is probably safe to steer a midway course, marked by the buoys of actual fact. Experience shows that an era of active gold production may be accompanied by a fall in the prices of commodities, either because the multiplication of commodities may be progressing more rapidly than the output of gold, or because inactivity of trade, perhaps due to some shock to credit, may be checking the demand for commodities. But when the more normal effect of increased gold supplies is at work, and the prices of goods are rising, the producers of the goods are thereby benefited, and set to work harder than ever to produce them. The mechanism of transport is extended and improved, the waste places of the earth are ploughed

* Vol. i. ch. i. § 33.

and watered, and the material heritage of mankind is increased and multiplied. So much so that the demand for credit and capital for the furtherance of these extensions is apt to become so keen, that, as we saw in the recent period of great commercial expansion, an era of active gold production may coincide with high rates for money.

It is thus evident that innumerable and incalculable considerations have to be enumerated and calculated before we can say with certainty either that variations in the amount of gold are of no importance, or that they will have results which can be definitely counted on. But for the purposes of our present inquiry there is no need to wonder what might happen if the available gold supply were doubled; it may be asserted that, rightly or wrongly, and up to a certain point, if any reasonably possible addition was made to the Bank of England's store of gold, the event would, in normal times, be welcomed by the commercial community. The position of the Bank would be regarded as stronger, the City would be cheerful and optimistic, and there would be so much more credit available for any borrower who had an enterprise to finance and could give good security. If there were no enterprising borrowers with good security to offer, the new gold would certainly be useless. But, except in times of extreme slackness in trade, this is an improbable contingency; and it also is improbable that extreme slackness in trade would last long, if it were treated with sufficient doses of this medicine.

We are thus wandering far afield from our consideration of sovereigns in the pocket to gold as the basis of credit. But these monetary questions are all so inextricably entangled that it is almost impossible to mark them off logically and deal with them one by one. It is the universal acceptability of gold in civilized communities that gives it both its popularity in the shape of sovereigns, and its importance as a wheel in the machinery of credit. And this importance is so great that it had to be referred to on our first meeting with the metal in the course of this inquiry.

The small change that we carry in our purses need not detain us long. It must be noted that silver coins are not "legal tender" to the extent of more than £2; that is to say, if you owe your tailor £5, you cannot legally satisfy the debt by handing him one hundred shillings or any other arrangement in silver. Probably it would not occur to you to do so, and if you did he would probably accept it, and the restriction is not apparently of much practical importance. Actually it is most important, for the dreary record of currency history is a long tale of the uncertainty and inconvenience which arose in the days when people tried to keep gold and silver circulating on equal terms at a fixed ratio, with the result that the one which happened for the moment to be less valuable as bullion continually drove out of circulation the one which was more valuable, thanks to the operation of Gresham's Law * and the quick and cunning bullion merchants. Bimetallists maintain that the confusion and difficulty of the two-metal system only arose because it was not scientifically and universally applied, and Bimetallism has been endorsed by eminent theoretical authority. The simplicity of the single standard, however, has obvious practical advantages, and it may at least be claimed that England, by making silver legal tender only up to sums of £2, and adopting what is called a gold standard, solved a problem which had puzzled the civilized world for centuries.

It may also be observed that our silver coins are mere tokens; that is to say, they do not pretend to contain as much of the metal as would, if melted down, fetch as much as the value at which they circulate. At the present moment † there is roughly about fourpennyworth of silver in a shilling, which thus has a purely conventional and artificial value as currency.

Bronze coins are legal tender only to the extent of one shilling.

* See p. 14. † December, 1908.

CHAPTER III

PAPER CASH

THE exchange of a hat for a sovereign is a quite commonplace proceeding, but when we begin to exchange a hat for a piece of paper, which is only accepted because it is believed to be convertible into gold, the element of belief, that is to say of credit, enters into the transaction, and we have moved up a step on the ladder of economic civilization.

The first stage, as we have seen, was from barter, by which goods were exchanged for goods, to purchase, by which goods were exchanged for one commodity of universal acceptability. And a process of painful evolution finally decided that gold was best fitted to be that commodity. But an enormous expansion of trade was made possible when it was discovered that gold could be economized by the use of paper which represented and multiplied it, and when confidence in a banker became sufficiently established to induce the community to circulate his promises to pay instead of pieces of metal.

The process of this evolution, also, was painful enough, and the loss and uncertainty caused by the bad and debased coin currency of the Middle Ages were rivalled by the ruin and disasters of the early days of banking, when notes were issued without any regard for the assets which were behind them, or the ability of the issuer to meet them on presentation. Nevertheless, the appearance of the bank-note marks the first step in the development of banking as we understand it nowadays, that is, of a machinery for the manufacture of credit.

Before the bank-note won its way into circulation, such bankers as existed were chiefly goldsmiths and bullion dealers; they were sometimes loan mongers, collecting coin from one set of customers to lend it to another, or to discount bills for another, but it was only when they began to induce those who borrowed from them to take the cash advanced in the form of notes that the economy of metal became possible and the wheel of the credit machine began to turn to any purpose. The original goldsmith's note was a receipt for metal deposited. It took the form of a promise to pay metal, and so passed as currency. Some ingenious goldsmith conceived the epoch-making notion of giving notes, not only to those who had deposited metal, but to those who came to borrow it, and so founded modern banking.

As long as the bankers took care of coin and

ingots for Jones and lent them to Smith, the commercial community was given a certain convenience, by knowing where dealers in money were to be found, but the convenience was severely restricted. When the bankers lent Smith not coin but a promise to pay coin, they soon discovered, since their promise to pay did not at once come back to them for presentation, that in the mean time they might safely accommodate Brown, Robinson and Williams with a similar number of similar promises to pay; and so they hit on the great device by which modern commerce transacts its business by means of evidence of mutual indebtedness between it and its bankers.

At first sight there is something whimsical in the process of stimulating production and expanding trade by an agreement between two parties to owe one another something; but this agreement is an important part of the structure of the modern edifice of credit.

Let us see it at work in the case of the primitive bank which we are now supposing to be emerging from the bullion-dealing to the note-issuing stage. At first, we supposed it engaged in taking care of metallic money for Smith and lending it to Jones, and its balance-sheet would stand thus, if we leave out its capital for the sake of simplicity:—

Due to Smith . .	£10,000	Loan to Jones . .	£10,000

After it had made the momentous step of inducing Jones to take its notes instead of metal, the balance-sheet would show the following development:—

Due to Smith	£10,000	Cash in hand	£10,000
Notes outstanding	10,000	Loan to Jones	10,000
Total	£20,000	Total	£20,000

You will observe that since Jones has taken his loan in notes the cash originally deposited by Smith remains in the bank's hands, and the loan to Jones is represented by a liability of the bank to meet the notes which it has passed over to him. These notes, being a promise to pay by the bank, are in effect a loan by Jones to it, and thus Jones and the bank have become mutually indebted. The bank has lent £10,000 to Jones, and he, by taking payment in the bank's promises to pay, is lending it £10,000 as long as he refrains from presenting the notes and demanding cash for them. Jones and the bank are thus mutually indebted, and by their agreement to owe one another money the currency has been increased by £10,000, and to that extent Jones is enabled to hire and load a ship for foreign trade, or otherwise to engage in productive enterprise.

When the bank finds that the notes which Jones borrowed are not quickly presented, but are accepted by the commercial community for the payments that he makes in loading his ship, and passed on from hand to hand and remain outstanding, it proceeds to the next step of making advances to Brown, Robinson and Williams, and the balance-sheet will be amplified as follows:—

Due to Smith .	£10,000	Cash in hand .	£10,000
Notes outstanding	40,000	Loans to customers	40,000
	£50,000		£50,000

The great principle of currency based on mutual indebtedness has thus been extended; the bank is liable for £40,000 of its promises to pay on demand, and its customers are indebted to it for £40,000. And this £40,000 is in circulation, quickening the wheels of trade, increasing production and profitable commerce. And the mutual indebtedness of the bank and its customers has brought this new currency into being.

But it will be observed that the bank now owes £50,000 in all, and holds only £10,000 in metallic cash against all these liabilities on demand. This will probably be a safe proportion for it to work on in ordinary circumstances, but if it continued to increase the amount of its note issue without a proportionate increase in the amount of cash held against it, the day would come when some unforeseen accident brought in an unusual number of notes for presentation, and its fate would be sealed. In the early days of banking this sort of disaster was common enough, and folk found that they had sold their goods and services in return for notes which they had believed to be as good as gold and discovered too late to be worth only the paper that they were printed on. The manufacture of currency out of mutual indebtedness had proved too easy and simple a process, and the necessity for a proportionate backing of gold had been ignored.

Disasters of this kind not only reduced the number of note-issuing banks in England, but produced a body of opinion which aimed at making the bank-note a mere bullion certificate, only to be issued against a backing of gold to its full value. In London, the Bank of England had, since its very early days, possessed the monopoly of note issue as far as joint-stock companies were concerned, and the private banks had already ceased to issue notes when the question of the regulation of the note issue was taken in hand in 1844.

The body of opinion above referred to then prevailed, and it was decided by the Bank Act of 1844 that in future any expansion in the Bank of England's note circulation must only be based on metal. Up to £14,000,000 it might issue notes against securities, and it was arranged that if any country note issues lapsed, two-thirds of them might be added to the amount of notes that the

Bank of England might so issue, and this arrangement has since then raised the amount of bank-notes based on securities to nearly 18½ millions. By the terms of the Act, the metal held against any notes that might be issued above this line might be four-fifths gold and one-fifth silver; but the Bank has long ceased to hold silver against its notes, and any increase in their amount can now only be based on an increase in its gold store.

Such are the conditions under which Bank of England notes are now issued, and since country issues are in these days a small item in the volume of currency in England, the only notes that need here be considered are those of the Bank of England, which are, like sovereigns, legal tender to any amount. The value of a bank-note arises from the belief that it can be converted into gold and will be accepted as payment for goods. It therefore follows that since the Bank of England note is legal tender in England, it will be accepted in payment for goods as long as the British Government is strong enough to enforce the law of the land; and it is obvious that it can be converted into gold as long as the Bank of England is solvent, that is to say, keeps sufficient gold in its vaults to meet its notes on presentation; and it is compelled to keep the gold equivalent of every note that it issues above the £18,450,000, which it is allowed to issue against Government securities. The strength of the

Bank of England note thus depends on the power of the British Government to enforce the law, and on the solvency of the Bank of England. It is thus as strong as any mere promise to pay can be made, and is, for practical currency purposes, as good as gold.

The consideration of the bank-note has thus already taken us over the wavy and very ill-defined line which separates cash from credit. For a bank-note is both. It is cash in that it is immediately convertible into gold, and it is credit in that it is a promise to pay, and is only acceptable in payment for goods because it is believed to be as good as gold. Its use, in economizing gold and multiplying the effectiveness of the gold retained in the hands of the banker, has already been demonstrated, and it has also been recorded that the disasters which followed from its abuse, in days when bankers had not grasped the necessity for keeping an adequate proportion of gold to meet notes presented, and for keeping the rest of their assets liquid and realizable, led to a reaction. This reaction prompted the passing of measures in England which prohibited this economy of gold by means of the bank-note, and laid down that any increase in the Bank of England's issue was to be based on an equal amount of gold in its vaults, each £5-note being actually represented by £5 in gold.

If the apparent intentions of the Act of 1844 had been carried out, the subsequent enormous development of English trade, if it had been possible at all, must have been accompanied by the heaping up of a vast mass of gold in the Bank's vaults. But its intentions were evaded by the commercial community, which had already appreciated the advantages of a currency based on mutual indebtedness between itself and the banks. The commercial community ceased to circulate bank-notes under the new restrictions, developing the use for daily cash transactions of a credit instrument which had already acquired some popularity, namely, a draft or bill on its bankers payable on demand, and now commonly called a cheque. The drawing of cheques was not in any way limited by the Act of 1844, and the cheque was in many ways a more convenient form of currency than the bank-note. For the strength of the Bank of England note was in itself an inconvenience in one respect; since the nature of the note is such that any one who holds it can present it and be paid in gold for it at sight, a roll of them in one's pocket is as valuable a burden as so many sovereigns or gold bars, with the additional merit of being more easily carried by the owner, and the serious disadvantage of being more easily carried off by any one else. This danger is avoided or enormously reduced when the community adopts the habit, not of carrying or sending bank-notes, but of drawing a cheque on its bank for every transaction that it wishes to complete by payment.

The use of the cheque, however, involves the element of belief to a much greater extent than that of the bank-note. We have seen that the latter is certain of being taken in payment for goods or converted into gold as long as the British Government stands and the Bank of England is solvent, but the exchangeability of the former depends on the solvency of the drawer of the cheque—probably a private individual—and of the bank on which it is drawn. A shopkeeper who takes a cheque in payment for a pair of boots is liable on presenting it through his banker to have it returned marked with ominous signs, which are interpreted to mean that the customer's alleged bank refuses to meet it, because his account is overdrawn, or perhaps because he never had an account with it at all. Or it is barely possible that he may be informed that the bank on which the cheque was drawn has put up its shutters, though this possibility is happily one that need not be practically considered in these days, owing to the stability which centuries of experience and the light of publicity have given to British banking.

But these two risks, one a practical one and the other theoretically in being, make the extensive use of cheques possible only in a community which has reached a high stage of economic civilization, and is also blessed with a high level of general honesty among its members. And these features in the character of a cheque also made it obviously impossible that it could be given the privilege of legal tender, that is, that any one could be bound by law to accept a cheque in payment for goods delivered or services rendered. No one could be compelled to take a piece of paper signed by an unknown person and purporting to be an order on a bank of which perhaps he had never heard. So that the cheque has had to fight its way to its present supremacy without this advantage, and to drive gold and notes out of circulation, except in small and special transactions, in spite of the fact that they were legal tender and it was not. This it was enabled to do by its safety and convenience, and the power of the drawer, by varying the form in which he makes it out, to hedge it about with safeguarding restrictions, or to leave it convertible into cash by any one who presents it. A cheque is merely an order on a bank from one of its customers to pay some of the money which it holds on his account to a third party, or to himself if he wants to take out cash. It can be manufactured with a piece of notepaper and a penny stamp, but it is much more usual to use one of the well-known regular forms supplied by banks to their customers.

The convenience of the cheque follows from its safety; if bank-notes are being sent, it is necessary to note all the numbers and register the packet; a cheque, protected by being crossed and marked "not negotiable," goes safely in an ordinary envelope. The words "not negotiable" do not make a cheque not negotiable, but their effect is, that no holder of a cheque so marked can pass on a better title to it than he has himself; consequently, if it is stolen, any one who takes it from the thief cannot claim on it. Further, the fact that it can be drawn to the exact amount required is a great advantage, and its return to the drawer through his bank, when it has done its work and been cancelled, is an additional convenience, and makes the cheque a record and receipt, as well as a form of payment.

But in considering the qualities of the cheque it must never be forgotten that it also, like the Bank of England note, is a certificate immediately convertible into legal tender cash, gold or notes. It need hardly be said that the great majority of cheques are never presented to be turned into cash; they are paid into banks by those who receive them, and crossed off against one another in the Clearing-house, where representatives of all the banks meet and exchange claims against one another; and cheques thus for the most part merely act as indicators in the transactions which result in the daily transfer of an enormous amount of credit from one hand to another, the whole affair being finally reduced to a matter of book-keeping exchanges between the various bankers and between the various accounts in their books. But the fact that every cheque gives the holder, or his bank, the right to demand legal tender, gold or notes, from the bank on which it is drawn is highly important; without it, the cheque could not have won its way to general acceptability, and could not be treated as cash, as it is rather heretically treated here, on the ground that it is, in the vast majority of cases, readily accepted in exchange for goods or services in ordinary transactions. And the immediate convertibility into gold or notes, which is behind every cheque, means that an adequate supply of gold or notes to meet them on presentation is as necessary to bankers who supply their customers with cheque-books as to those who formerly made advances to them in the shape of notes, or promises to pay. In these days when a banker lends money, he lends the right to draw a cheque and promises to meet it on demand, so that the principle of mutual indebtedness as part of the basis of modern commercial currency is again evident. And since the right to draw a cheque implies the right to call for gold or notes, the extent to which credit can be created by bankers will depend, among other things, on the amount of gold or notes that bankers hold against possible demands. A banker who has £10,000 in gold or notes at his command would be running too great a banking risk if he advanced ten millions to the most unexceptionable customers against the most unexceptionable securities; for by doing so he would give them the right to take out ten millions in gold and notes, and if even a thousandth part of the right were exercised, the banker's gold and notes would all be gone. And since, as we have seen, notes are mere bullion certificates, themselves immediately convertible into gold, we come back to gold as an element of first importance in the creation of banking credit. Or we can express the matter more simply by saying that the amount of gold held by the banking community as a whole will be a leading influence among those which determine the amount of the cheques that it can allow the commercial and financial community, as a whole, to draw. All this is perhaps a little premature in a chapter which purports to be dealing with cash transactions. But the cheque, like the bank-note, is at once cash and credit, and it cannot be too early stated and understood that every credit operation implies a possible cash transaction, and that prudent banking consists in making due allowance for cash demands involved by the creation of credit.

CHAPTER IV

THE BILL OF EXCHANGE

HAVING reviewed the various forms of cash, or money here and now, for which goods and services are habitually exchanged, and for which the money market exchanges money some day or money somewhere else, we proceed to the bill of exchange, a versatile credit instrument which is often all these three forms of money in the course of its career. The complicated relations between the different kinds of money, and their habit of melting into another, are well exemplified when it is stated that the cheque, with which we are supposed to have already dealt, is actually nothing else but a bill of exchange, with which we now propose to deal.

But there is this difference. A cheque is a bill of exchange payable on demand. A bill of exchange, as we shall see, is an order from A to B to pay a sum either to himself, A, or to a third party, C. When it is payable forthwith it is a cheque and bears a penny stamp; when it is payable at a future date it is a bill of exchange and bears a stamp *ad valorem*, varying with the amount of the sum named. It is characteristic of monetary nomenclature, which seems to try to confuse matters by applying illogical and confusing names, that the title "bill of exchange" should be given both to the genus and to one of the species into which it is divided. Another distinction exists in the eye of the law, from the fact that a cheque, according to its legal definition, must be drawn on a bank, whereas a bill may be drawn on a bank but is more often drawn on a merchant or accepting house, or any debtor who gives his creditor the right to draw on him. The practice of the market-place, however, does not always follow the legal definition of the cheque, but applies the word to any bill payable on demand. The element of time is thus the real outstanding quality in the bill of exchange, which separates it from the cheque and justifies my reservation of it to a separate chapter apart from the forms of paper cash.

Logically, the reasons which included cheques under the category of cash would perhaps include the bill of exchange. Goods and services are constantly given in exchange for bills, and a good bill, drawn on an English bank or firm, is convertible into gold. But it has to go through two important processes before it can be so converted. It has to be accepted, and it has either to be discounted or to await maturity.

The bill of exchange is of immemorial antiquity. "It is probable," says a great authority on its legal aspects, "that a bill of exchange was in its original nothing more than a letter of credit from a merchant in one country to his debtor, a merchant in another, requiring him to pay the debt to a third person, who carried the letter, and happened to be travelling to the place where the debtor resided. . . . It was found that the original bearer might often with advantage transfer it to another, and the assignee was, perhaps, desirous to know, beforehand, whether the party to whom it was addressed, would pay it and sometimes showed it to him for that purpose; his promise to pay was the origin of acceptances." *

It is obvious from this theoretical description of the early bill that it, like its modern descendant, was not immediately payable, since otherwise its bearer would most obviously and simply have tested the willingness to pay of the merchant on whom it was drawn, by presenting it for payment. Acceptance is nothing else than the promise of the party on whom the bill is drawn that he will pay it at due date; and this acceptance he signifies by writing his name across the face of it. A cheque, in its legal sense, drawn on a bank, does not require acceptance, because its payment constitutes and includes its acceptance; but a cheque, in the sense

* Byles on Bills of Exchange.

of a bill payable on demand, drawn on a firm which is not a bank, is often accepted

It is rather astonishing to find the authority just referred to stating that there is no evidence that bills of exchange were in use among the ancients, though he refers to a passage in Cicero's letters which appears, to a lay mind, to establish the fact beyond doubt. Writing to Atticus,* Cicero asks him to consider whether the monetary requirements of his son at Athens can be provided by exchange operations, and it is interesting to see that the Latin phrase is a literal counterpart of the English—*permutari.* But although this passage is not sufficient evidence, from a legal point of view, that such a thing as a bill of exchange was used, it clearly proves the existence of some form of exchange machinery in Rome and Athens; and it is safe to assume that the acute and quick-minded Greeks exchanged credits against the goods that they bought and sold between their busy cities.

The precise age of the bill of exchange, however, is a question of merely antiquarian interest. We are now concerned with its meaning and the function that it performs in the monetary machine. It is legally defined as "an unconditional order in writing addressed by one person to another, signed by the person giving it, requiring the person to whom it is addressed to pay on demand, or at a

* Cic. *ad Att.*, 12, 24.

fixed or determinable future time, a certain sum in money to, or to the order of, a specified person, or to bearer."

Thus says the law. But, as we have already seen, a bill of exchange becomes a cheque, in practice and in the eye of the tax-gatherer, when it is payable on demand; and in the eye of the law likewise when it is payable on demand and drawn on a bank. So that the distinctive part of its actual definition consists in its being payable at a future date. Further, though it may be an order drawn by one party on another in the same street, nevertheless, since trade consists largely in the exchange of goods between persons separated by distance, it is usual to find that bills of exchange are drawn by the merchants or financiers of one centre on those of another. In other words, time is a constant element in the composition of a bill of exchange, and space is a very usual one. When Sancho Panza had his ass stolen by a ruffian whom his master's chivalry had set free from the grip of the law, Don Quixote consoled him with a promise of a bill of exchange (*cédula di cambio*) for three asses out of five in his stable. As they were then wandering in the Sierra Morena, the elements of time and space were both present. The bill was duly drawn on Don Quixote's niece, and ran as follows:—

"Dear niece,—At sight of this, my first bill of

ass-colts, give order that three out of the five I left at home in your custody be delivered to Sancho Panza, my squire; which three colts I order to be delivered and paid for the like number received of him here in tale; and this, with his acquittance, shall be your discharge. Done in the heart of the Sierra Morena, the twenty-second of August, this present year——"

"It is mighty well," said Sancho, "now you have only to sign it."

"It wants no signing," said Don Quixote; "I need only put my cipher to it, which is the same thing, and is sufficient, not only for three, but for three hundred asses."

The draft was thus in many respects irregular; apart from the fact, with which the priest consoled Sancho when he found that he had lost it, that "one written in a pocket-book would not be accepted." Nevertheless, this bill drawn in jest by Cervantes on posterity more than three centuries ago, is a very fair parody of its modern counterpart. Its verbiage, of course, has been left out, the bill of to-day being generally drawn with business-like brevity; but it is a definite order to Don Quixote's niece, signed by his cipher, to pay a stated number of ass-colts, to Sancho, against value received from him at the place where the bill is drawn. The fact that this value received is wholly fictitious is not quite without parallel in modern practice. Modern practice, in its insatiable search for means of credit manufacture, has often found it convenient to create bills of exchange out of nothing, drawing them against aspirations or expectations or speculations. And cases have been known in which an attempt was made to give the "kites," or accommodation paper, so produced, an air of demure respectability by some reference to goods passing, as imaginary as the three asses which Don Quixote states that he has received from Sancho.

The original essence of a bill of exchange was that it was a claim for the payment of a debt, based on the moving of saleable produce to the place at which it is expected to find a market. The custom which made it payable at a date subsequent to its arrival, and the arrival of the goods, was presumably arranged in order to give the merchant who received them, and owed the money for them, time to dispose of them and garner the proceeds. But his acceptance of the bill, or acknowledgment that he has to pay the money at its date of maturity, makes it immediately negotiable, or convertible into cash, by the process of discount, which will be explained later.

Let us take a concrete example, and simplify it by the elimination of many of the processes through which a modern bill actually passes.

Silas P. Watt, farmer, of Dakota, sells his

wheat-crop for £2000 to John Smith, of London, corn-dealer; John Smith sees no reason why he should pay for the wheat before it has been shipped, knowing that a month or two must pass before it has reached him, and been marketed and turned into money in his pocket. Silas P. Watt, on the other hand, sees no reason why, during all this interval, he should have parted with his wheat and should have nothing to show for it; and his banker or trust-manager, who has probably made an advance against it, is even more strongly convinced of the impropriety of such a proceeding. Consequently, thanks to the compromise which commerce has devised to meet this difficulty, Watt in Dakota draws a bill on Smith in London for £2000 payable at sixty days' sight, and is able to give this bill to his bank or trust company to be realized in payment for the loan on his crop. The bank endorses the bill by signing its name on the back of it, and sends it to its agent in London, together with documents showing that the wheat has been actually shipped and insured against risks on the way, and on its arrival it is accepted by Smith, who writes his signature across the front of it to show that he acknowledges the indebtedness at the due date, and is given possession of the documents. It is thereupon, supposing Smith's name to be good and in sound credit, a negotiable instrument which can be discounted, that is, turned into as much ready cash as a promise to pay at a distant date is worth according to the current rate of interest. For example, if the £2000 bill has still a month to run and the current rate of interest is 6 per cent. per annum, its present value will be decided by simple arithmetic to be £1990.

This is a very simple example of the manner in which the bill of exchange facilitates trade by creating a piece of negotiable paper against a genuine trade transaction. Wheat was not wanted in Dakota, and is always wanted in London, and therefore its transfer from Dakota to London gives it value by putting it into the place in which it will fetch a price. The interval is bridged by the bill, which finances the transaction from its beginning to its end. When the bill falls due, if, as we may suppose for the sake of clearness, it has not been discounted, Watt or his bank (to whom we suppose him to have passed it on) applies through his London agent to Smith for the money, and Smith having in the meantime disposed of the wheat is in a position to give his cheque for the amount; the agent cashes the cheque and places the proceeds to the credit of the bank in London, to be used as it may direct. In actual practice, however, the bank's agent would probably have discounted the bill and so turned it into immediate cash on its arrival, and the bank in Dakota would already have sold drafts on London against it, to customers in America who had payments to make in England.

A bill, such as this one that we have imagined, drawn against the actual shipment of actual produce, and especially of produce of universal demand and immediate consumption, such as wheat, obviously possesses the great advantage of "paying itself," according to the common phrase in Lombard Street. The wheat comes to market and is sold, and cancels the debt created against it.

It thus begins to appear that the bill of exchange is not only a beautifully simple and efficacious device for financing commerce, but is also an ideal form of investment for bankers and others who are obliged by the nature of their business to keep their resources liquid, that is, readily convertible into cash.

For a genuine bill of the kind described pays itself automatically, as we have seen, at maturity, owing to the necessities of the community, which must have wheat or perish, and a banker who invests his funds by discounting good bills has only to let some of his bills mature without replacing them, in order to replenish his store of cash. Bills drawn against wool, cotton, hides, and other raw materials of the principal industries which are turned into articles of universal consumption are, for practical purposes, equally good; for the goods behind the bill, being certain of a market, and likely, if anything, to rise in value in time of war or political scare, secure the acceptor against the chance of being "locked up," as it is called, with an asset which he cannot realize.

It is this quality, inherent in a genuine bill, which gave rise to the saying that banking is the easiest possible business to conduct, when once the banker has grasped the difference between a bill of exchange and a mortgage. We have seen that the genuine bill of exchange is easily negotiable before maturity, and on maturity is cash by the sale of the goods on which it is based. A mortgage or loan against real property, houses and land, is by no means readily negotiable, since the two expensive processes of survey and examination of title are involved before it can be transferred, and the security behind it is the most difficult of all to turn into cash, especially at times of political or other disturbance. "You may buy land now as cheap as stinking mackerel," says Falstaff, when he brings news of Hotspur's rebellion.

But, as a matter of practical fact, a very large number of the bills drawn are not of this genuine character, and the use of this admirable and efficient instrument of credit has been so extended, that the distinction between it and a mortgage on real property is nowadays sometimes in favour of the latter, which has at any rate something behind it.

We have seen that the original justification of a bill of exchange arose from its being drawn against produce in the course of being marketed, or being worked up into a state in which it would be more valuable, and that the bill bridged the intermediate period by providing the buyer and seller with an instrument that could be immediately realized. A very short step in advance of this arrangement led the dealers in exchange to create bills at a time of year when no crops were ready to be drawn against, in order to make profits out of the provision of a form of remittance at these periods, and to cover themselves later on when the genuine produce bills began to come forward. Let us once more take a concrete case. In July, Silas Watt may want to make a payment in London for farming machinery ; he has no crop to draw against as yet, but his banker will sell him a draft on London, having made arrangements with Smith, who is now grown from a merchant into an "accepting house," to accept bills drawn by it, for a consideration, against securities instead of produce. When Watt's crop is harvested, and a genuine bill on London is created by its sale, it will restore the American bank's credits in London, which were reduced by the draft that it had provided to pay for Watt's machinery.

When John Smith is described as having grown from a merchant into an accepting house, he is supposed to have passed through a process which has been a fairly common experience. Like many other merchant houses, he has given up the actual handling and selling of merchandise, though retaining the title of merchant, which is highly honoured in the City, and is confining his attention to the profits which he can more easily earn, if his name be good enough, by placing his acceptance at the disposal of borrowers who want to draw on him. The arrangement that he has made with Watt's banker, and with many other dealers in bills of exchange in other parts of the world, enables them to draw on one another at any time, whether there be produce passing or no, and brings into being the instrument known as a finance bill. By this operation he and they create credit instruments which can be discounted and turned into cash, on the security of their names which are on the bills.

This system of creating bills of exchange, as long as they are created in anticipation of crop movements and other genuine processes by which products are given value by treatment and movement into the place where they are wanted, is quite legitimate, and tends, as will be explained in a later chapter, to steady the fluctuations in exchange, and to check unnecessary shipments of gold backwards and forwards across the hemispheres.

But having discovered that profitable business was to be done by creating bills in anticipation of movements of produce or manufactures, the enterprising spirits of the financial community were naturally impelled to go further, and create bills for the mere purpose of discounting them and so providing themselves with cash. As there was no moving produce in question, they were created against property that would be difficult of realization, such as landed estate, or against securities which might or might not be easy to sell, or merely against the credit of the creators, and all the varieties of bills so produced differ more or less essentially from the ideal form of bill of exchange, which, as we saw, paid itself on maturity by being drawn against actual movements of produce of general and rapid consumption. The dangers involved by the abuse of the ease with which bills can be created are increased by the great difficulty of detecting from the appearance of a bill whether there be real produce behind it, or some other form of security, or nothing but the credit of the parties. Some bills carry on their faces a history of the whole transaction involved. Subjoined is a specimen, faithfully copied, with names altered :—

LAING, MACKAY & Co.

No. 406.

EXCHANGE FOR £169 · 4 · 6 *Stg.* *Madras,* 11*th June* 1908

Three months after sight of this first of Exchange (second and third of same tenor and date not paid) pay to the Credit Bank of India *or order* Pounds One hundred and sixty nine, shillings four, and pence six *Sterling, value received, and place the same to account as advised.*

Of 50 Bs. Hemp, per s.s. Napoleon to Bremen.

To Messrs. John Smith & Co.,
London.

LAING, MACKAY & Co.

More commonly these details are omitted, and the bill takes a form like this:—

Evans and Pugh.

£2000. NEW YORK, *Sept. 3rd*, 1908.

At ninety days after sight of this FIRST of Exchange (SECOND Unpaid) pay to the order of Messrs. Jones.

TWO THOUSAND POUNDS STERLING,
Value received, and charge the same to a/c as advised.

To John Smith & Co.
London. EVANS & PUGH.

Experts in credit, with a mass of collateral evidence at the back of their heads, may be able to hazard a shrewd guess from the appearance of a bill, as to what is behind it. But the phrase "Value received" covers a multitude of mystery, and the difference between a genuine produce bill and a piece of finance paper is often difficult to detect. Finance bills being based on securities which are less readily realizable, especially in times of apprehension and uncertainty, than genuine produce of general demand, are obviously more likely to land their acceptors in difficulty if they have been accepting too many of them. And it is thus easy to understand why, when there is any strain on credit, Lombard Street sometimes begins to talk seriously about the number of finance bills that are passing.

Another class of bill that becomes unpopular when the market for credit is in a nervous state is the "house bill," that is, the bill drawn by a firm or company on itself. If, for example, John Smith establishes his brother Robert in Oporto to finance the port wine trade, and the Oporto Smith draws bills extensively on Smith in London, being merely an oversea branch of the same firm, the bills so drawn will not be as good as if they were drawn by one firm on another which is wholly distinct, and so carried behind them the credit and resources of two establishments. If this paper became too common, the watch-dogs of the credit organization would remark that there was too much Smith on Smith about, and would describe it, in its picturesque phrase, as mere "pig on pork."

The classical example of pig on pork is the order on Mrs. Micawber which Mr. Micawber gave to David Copperfield in the King's Bench prison. "Mr. Micawber," so David tells the tale, "was waiting for me within the gate, and went up to his room (top story but one) and cried very much. He solemnly conjured me, I remember, to take warning by his fate; and to observe that if a man had twenty pounds a year for his income, and spent nineteen pounds nineteen shillings and sixpence, he would be happy, but that if he spent twenty pounds one he would be miserable. After which he borrowed a shilling of me for porter, gave me a written order on Mrs. Micawber for the amount, and put away his pocket handkerchief and cheered up."

David would have found some difficulty in

inducing anybody to discount that bill, though doubtless Mrs. Micawber would have accepted it with a fine flourish, and with perfect confidence that "something would turn up" before it was presented. Nevertheless its complete worthlessness has been parallelled before now in the world of commercial fact, when foreign firms have established branches, consisting of a clerk and an office boy, in England, and drawn bills on them, which have been accepted, of course, by the clerk, who had authority to sign for the firm by procuration, and have then actually been discounted and turned into cash.

Mr. Micawber has thus taken us a step further than Don Quixote. The Don drew a bill on his niece, whom he knew to be able and ready to meet it, in favour of Sancho, against a fictitious delivery by Sancho to him of three ass-colts. Micawber, in a debtors' prison, drew in favour of David on his wife, who was then in process of being sold up. He doubtless believed, nay was certain, that his paper was as good as gold. So do many others who draw on a branch establishment which possesses nothing but an office table; and this Micawberish optimism is at the back of a good deal of the exuberant energy which makes trade hum in times of activity. And consequently when trade slackens, and folk begin to consider sceptically concerning the basis of the credit that has been built up during the humming period, there are sometimes some awkward moments of surprise and disillusionment.

The importance of the bill of exchange thus lies in a merit and a danger attached to it. The merit is the fact that in its genuine form it facilitates trade by creating credits and so supplying cash against real produce not yet marketed, and is also an ideal form of investment for those whose investments must be liquid, or certain of easy realization. The danger is the ease with which it can be created against securities which may not be readily marketable, or by being drawn on firms by themselves, or by correspondents, in order to provide cash for speculative enterprise.

CHAPTER V

THE MANUFACTURE OF MONEY

HAVING reviewed the various forms of cash, or money here and now, and the bill of exchange, which, from its ready negotiability and from its becoming cash on maturity, may be described as very nearly cash, we may pause and look back over the ground already traversed.

We saw that gold, with auxiliary tokens of silver and bronze, is still the cash of the pocket for retail transactions, but that its use in big commercial and financial transactions was economized first by the use of bank-notes, and then, when the law laid restrictions on the use of bank-notes which prevented any increase in their issue except against an equal amount of gold, by the use of cheques. But we found that the general acceptability of notes and cheques arose from their being convertible into gold, which is the only form of payment that is universally and always acceptable in the economically civilized world.

The restrictions on the bank-note have practically eliminated note issues in England except that of the

Bank of England note, which being legal tender and backed by the gold in the bank's vaults is regarded as a bullion certificate just as good as gold, and has become itself part of the basis of credit. That is to say, a banker who has Bank of England notes in his till is in a position to make advances to his customers on the strength of them, exactly as if they were sovereigns. The money of modern English commerce and finance is the cheque, and the credit dealt in in the London money market is the right to draw a cheque. We have next to find out how this right to draw a cheque is created, and we shall find that it is generally created by an advance made by a banker.

Since the cheque is an order to pay gold or notes, it is sometimes assumed that all these orders which are turned over by the London bankers' Clearing-house, to the extent of some thirty millions a day, are orders drawn by folk who have acquired the right to do so by depositing gold and notes with the banks. And it is a common popular mistake, when one is told that the banks of the United Kingdom hold over 900 millions of deposits, to open one's eyes in astonishment at the thought of this huge amount of cash that has been saved by the community as a whole, and stored by them in the hands of their bankers, and to regard it as a tremendous evidence of wealth.

But this is not quite the true view of the case.

Most of the money that is stored by the community in the banks consists of book-keeping credits lent to it by its bankers. It is usually supposed that bankers take money from one set of customers and then lend it to other customers; but in most cases, the money taken by one bank has been lent by another.

It will be remembered that when we were tracing the origin of the bank-note, we drew up an imaginary and simplified balance-sheet of a note-issuing bank showing—

Due to depositors	£10,000	Cash in hand ..	£10,000
Notes outstanding	40,000	Advances to customers	40,000
	£50,000		£50,000

In order to simplify the matter, we left out the bank's capital reserves, investments, and other items which appear in balance-sheets, but, now that we have come to the point at which the manufacture of the right to draw cheques has to be made as clear as may be, it will be better to come into closer touch with the facts of the case and look at a bank balance-sheet of to-day. In order to get a fair average specimen I have taken the latest available balance-sheets of half a dozen of the biggest banks, and put their figures together. But before we can consider them it will perhaps be safer, in the interests of clearness, to try to arrive at some rough notion of the meaning of a balance-sheet.

A balance-sheet is a statement showing on the left side the balances of the amounts that have been received, or are owing, by the company or firm that issues it; and on the right side the amounts that have been paid out by it, or are owing to it, or are held by it. On its left side are the liabilities, on the right the assets. If you are not well versed in these mysteries you will probably be astonished to see the banks' capital among their liabilities; but reflection will show that the capital was subscribed to the companies by their shareholders, to whom they have to account for it, and was invested in the assets on the other side. After this introduction to balance-sheets in general, let us examine the aggregated specimen that I have drawn up.

	Millions of £.		Millions of £.
Capital paid up	16	Cash in hand and at the Bank of England ..	43
Reserve Fund	11	Loans at call and short notice	27½
Current and deposit accounts	249	Bills discounted and advances	153
Acceptances on behalf of customers	16½	Investments	48
Profit and Loss account	1½	Liability of customers on acceptances	16½
		Premises	6
	294		294

The above statement does not include the figures

of the Bank of England, but is an agglomeration of the balance-sheets of six of the biggest of the ordinary joint-stock banks.

The first feature that strikes the casual observer is the smallness of the paid-up capital of the banks when compared with the vastness of the figures that they handle. We see that only 16 millions out of the 294 that they have to account for have been actually paid up by shareholders, though 11 millions have been retained out of past profits and accumulated in reserve funds, and 1½ millions are due to shareholders, for distribution as dividend or addition to reserve, in the shape of the profit and loss account balance for the period covered by the balance-sheet. A profit of 1½ millions on 16 is handsome enough, especially when it is considered that most of these balance-sheets covered a half-year's work, but 1½ millions out of 294 is a trifle, and it thus appears that a narrow margin of profit on their total turn-over enables the banks to pay good dividends, and that the business of credit manufacture earns its reward, as might be expected, out of the credit that it makes.

Proceeding in our examination, we see that the item of acceptances on behalf of customers on one side is balanced by the liability of customers on acceptances on the other. This means that the banks have accepted bills for their customers (so making them first-class paper and easily negotiable), and are so technically liable to meet them on maturity; but since the customers are expected to meet them, and have presumably given due security, this liability of the customer to the bank is an off-setting asset against the acceptance. And since the acceptance business is a comparatively small item, and a bank's liability under its acceptances is not a liability in quite the same sense as its deposits, and does not immediately affect the present question of the manufacture of currency, it may be omitted for the present. We can thus simplify the balance-sheet by taking out this contra entry on both sides.

Further analysis of the liabilities shows that the capital, reserves, and profit and loss balance may be regarded as due from the banks to their share-holders, and that the remaining big item, current and deposit accounts, is due to their customers. This is the item which is usually spoken of as the deposits, according to the tiresome habit of monetary nomenclature which seems to delight in applying the same name to a genus and one of the species into which it is divided. Just as the bill of exchange is divided into cheques and bills of exchange, so the banks' deposit accounts are divided into current and deposit accounts. But most people who have a banking account know the meaning of this distinction. Your current account is the amount at your credit which you can draw out, or against which you can draw cheques, at any moment; your deposit account is the amount that you have placed on deposit with the bank and can only withdraw on a week's or longer notice, and it earns a rate of interest, usually 1½ per cent. below the Bank of England's official rate. The essential point to be grasped is the fact that the banks' deposits, as usually spoken of, include both the current and deposit accounts, and are due by the banks to their customers.

Now let us see how this huge debt from the banks to the public has been created. An examination of the assets side of the balance-sheet proves that most of it has been created by money lent to their customers by the banks, and that the cheque currency of to-day is, like the note currency of a former day, based on mutual indebtedness between the banks and their customers. For the assets side shows that the banks hold 43 millions in cash and at the Bank of England, 48 millions in investments, and 6 millions invested in their premises—the buildings in which they conduct their business—and that 180½ millions have been lent by them to their customers, either by the discounting of bills or by advances to borrowers, or by loans at call or short notice. This last item is generally described in bank balance-sheets as "cash at call and short notice," but it has been lent, in most cases, to bill brokers, whose functions will be described later; and though more readily called in than the advances to ordinary customers, it has nevertheless been lent, and so seems to be hardly cash in the ordinary sense of the word. We can now reconstruct our balance-sheet, leaving out the acceptances on both sides, as follows:—

	Millions of £.		Millions of £.
Due to shareholders ..	28½	Cash in hand and at Bank of England	43
Due to customers ..	249	Investments	48
		Premises	6
		Due from customers ..	180½
	277½		277½

And it thus appears that nearly three-quarters of the amount due from the banks to their customers are due from their customers to the banks, having been borrowed from them in one form or another. And this proportion would perhaps be exceeded if we could take the figures of English banking as a whole. But that cannot be done at present, because some of the smaller banks do not separate their cash from their loans at call in their published statements. The greater part of the banks' deposits is thus seen to consist, not of cash paid in, but of credits borrowed. For every loan makes a deposit, and since our balance-sheet shows 180½ millions of loans, 180½ out of the 249 millions of deposits have been created by loans.

To take a concrete example, let us suppose that you want to buy a thousand-guinea motor-car and raise the wherewithal from your banker, pledging with him marketable securities, and receiving from him an advance, which is added to your current account. Being a prudent person you make this arrangement several days before you have to pay for the car, and so for this period the bank's deposits are swollen by your £1050, and on the other side of its balance-sheet the entry "advances to customers" is also increased by this amount, and the loan has clearly created a deposit.

But you raised your loan for a definite purpose, and not to leave with your bank, and it might be thought that when you use it to pay for your car the deposit would be cancelled. But not so. If the seller of your car banks at your bank, which we will suppose to be Parr's, he will pay your cheque into his own account, and Parr's bank's position with regard to its deposits will be unchanged, still showing the increase due to your loan. But if, as is obviously more probable, he banks elsewhere—perhaps at Lloyd's—he will pay your cheque into his account at Lloyd's bank, and it will be the creditor of Parr's for the amount of £1050. In actual fact, of course, so small a transaction would be swallowed up in the vast mass of the cross-entries which each of the banks every day makes against all the others, and would be a mere needle in a bottle of hay. But for the sake of clearness we will suppose that this little cheque is the only transaction between Parr's and Lloyd's on the day on which it is presented; the result would be that Parr's would transfer to Lloyd's £1050 of its balance at the Bank of England, where, as we shall see in a later chapter, all the banks keep an account for clearing purposes. And the final outcome of the operation would be that Parr's would have £1050 more "advances to customers" and £1050 less cash at the Bank of England among its assets, while Lloyd's would have £1050 more deposits and £1050 more cash at the Bank of England. But the £1050 increase in Lloyd's deposits would have been created by your loan, and though it will be drawn against by the man who sold you the car, it will only be transferred perhaps in smaller fragments to the deposits of other banks; and as long as your loan is outstanding there will be a deposit against it in the books of one bank or another, unless, as is most unlikely, it is used for the withdrawal of coin or notes; and even then the coin and notes are probably paid into some other bank, and become a deposit again; and so we come back to our original conclusion that your borrowing of £1050 has increased the sum of banking deposits, as a whole, by that amount.

The same reasoning applies whenever a bank

makes a loan, whatever be the collateral, whether Stock Exchange securities, as in the case cited, or bales of cotton or tons of copper; or, again, whenever it discounts a bill. In each case it gives the borrower or the seller of the bill a credit in its books—in other words, a deposit; and though this deposit is probably—almost certainly—transferred to another bank, the sum of banking deposits is thereby increased, and remains so, as long as the loans are in existence. And so it appears that the loans of one bank make the deposits of others, and its deposits consist largely of other banks' loans.

The matter is thus more complicated and difficult to follow under the system of banking by deposits and cheque-drawing than in the old days of note issue. When notes were the currency of commerce a bank which made an advance or discounted a bill gave its customer its own notes as the proceeds of the operation, and created a liability for itself. Now, a bank makes an advance or discounts a bill, and makes a liability for itself in the corresponding credit in its books; but this liability is in most cases almost immediately acted on and drawn against, and so transferred to another bank by being paid in as a deposit in the shape of a cheque on the lending bank. This cheque gives the bank which receives the deposit the right to so much of the lending bank's balance at the Bank of England, and the average result of the vast mass of credits so created and transferred roughly balances itself.

In order to try to see the process at work, let us take out all the loans, discounts, and advances from the balance-sheet on page 59, and the corresponding deposits, and then build them up again. Their excision would leave the balance-sheet, simplified in other respects, thus—

	Millions of £.		Millions of £.
Capital and reserves ..	27	Cash in hand and at the Bank	43
Profit and loss ..	1½	Investments	48
Current and deposit accounts	68½	Premises	6
	97		97

If, next day, each of the six banks lent ten millions which were drawn against and paid into one or other of the six, the aggregate of cash in hand and at the Bank would be unaltered, and the aggregate deposits would be increased by sixty millions, which would be represented by loans and advances on the other side, thus—

	Millions of £.		Millions of £.
Capital and reserves	27	Cash in hand and at the Bank	43
Profit and loss ..	1½	Investments	48
Current and deposit accounts	128½	Loans and advances ..	60
		Premises	6
	157		157

And so the process could be continued till we

arrived at the actual figures originally shown. The supposition that the operations would result in transfers between the six banks, and not to any of the others, makes our example look artificial, though if we could get an aggregate balance-sheet for all the banks, this supposition would be fact, though complicated by possible withdrawals of gold and notes, the amount of which would, however, be a small fraction of the total amounts transferred.

But perhaps we can make the matter clearer by eliminating the question of other banks, and their action and reaction on one another's position. Let us take the case of a little local bank with a complete monopoly of the banking business of a country town, in which it lends to every one who is in a position to borrow, and takes the deposits of every one who has a banking account. And let us suppose that this community is completely isolated, as far as money matters are concerned, from the rest of the country. We may draw up an imaginary and simplified balance-sheet for the bank as follows :—

	£		£
Capital	100,000	Cash in hand ..	200,000
Deposits	1,500,000	Investments ..	400,000
		Discounts and advances ..	1,000,000
	1,600,000		1,600,000

With these small and simple figures before us, and the conception in our minds of the small and compact community whose banking business they represent, it is easy to see the whole thing at work in imagination. The little town could not have deposited £1,500,000 without advances from the bank because there never was such a sum in the place. It has presumably deposited £100,000, since the bank holds £200,000 in cash, of which £100,000 may be taken as having been contributed by the subscribers of its capital. The rest of the deposits have been provided by the bank itself which, on the strength of its £200,000 of cash, has discounted bills for the local paper-mill and chair factory, and made advances against any securities or commodities that its customers had to borrow on and it considered good collateral, and has also given credits in its books for £400,000 against securities bought by it. The borrowers have probably been generally provided by the producing, manufacturing, and trading classes of the community, who have discounted bills and taken advances in order to finance themselves over the periods that necessarily elapse between outlay and realization in their various enterprises. This does not mean that their trade is unsound. They are earning regular profits; but before one profit is garnered they are at work in search of another, and borrowing the wherewithal to seek it; and by meeting their demands the bank is fulfilling the obvious and most useful business of a bank in financing production and industry. The land-holding, investing, and professional classes, who live ultimately on the producers and distributors, taking toll from them in the shape of rent, interest, and fees, probably do most of the depositing, paying back to the bank the cheques that they receive, drawn by those who acquired the right to draw by a discount, loan or overdraft. Part of the loans raised by the producers and distributors will be drawn out in coin for the payment of wages, and will work their way round, through the tills of the shopkeepers, back to the bank, when the shopkeepers pay in; for the retail dealers necessarily, from the nature of their trade, habitually deposit a considerable amount of currency with their bankers, while other people generally deposit cheques. And thus it appears that the banking credits provided by the bank for one set of customers, in the shape of loans and discounts, come back to it from another in the shape of deposits created by the loans and discounts.

In this case we see that a bank in this exceptional and monopolist position can, on a small cash basis, create, by discounting bills and making loans, the right to draw cheques, confident in the expectation that the cheques drawn by one customer will be paid into it by another; or that, on the rare occasions on which the right to draw is used by withdrawals of actual coin or notes, the coin or notes will find their way back to it, being deposited with it by those who receive them. And when its loans are repaid, or bills that it has discounted are met on maturity, this can only be done by the customers who have borrowed from it or taken bills to it for discount, paying it with a cheque on itself, and so cancelling a deposit; or perhaps by paying it in coin or notes, which they will get from some one who has cancelled a deposit in order to withdraw them. And so its loans and discounts create deposits when they are entered on, and cancel deposits when they mature, though in actual practice their place would more probably be taken by fresh loans or discounts.

From this parable of a little bank in an imaginary isolated community we can see how an exactly similar process works in English banking as a whole, though in its case the question is complicated by transfers from one bank to another. The historical evolution of the business tells the same tale. Banking in its note-issuing stage lent currency to its customers in the shape of its promissory notes, and had on the assets side its loans, and in the liabilities, its notes outstanding. It manufactured notes which it lent. Now, it manufactures credits in its books, and current and deposit accounts have taken the place of notes outstanding on the debit side of its balance-sheets.

It cannot conduct this manufacture without the

assistance of its customers, and it may be contended that these banking credits are manufactured, not by the banks, but by the customers who apply to them, and by the security that the customers bring, and the bankers approve of, as fit collateral. It is certainly true that the banks cannot make advances unless somebody asks for them, and their capacity for doing so thus depends on the needs of the community, and also on the supply of unpledged property that the community has available as security. Whether the manufacture be conducted by the banks or by their borrowing customers is a question of little moment, as long as the fact is grasped that the greater part of the deposits shown in bank balance-sheets have been brought into being by means of book-keeping credits—whether in the form of discounts, advances, or overdrafts—granted by banks to customers, and passed on by these customers to others.

The broad conclusion arrived at is that banking deposits come into being to a small extent by cash paid into banks across the counter, to a larger but still comparatively small extent by purchases of securities by the banks which create book credits, and chiefly by loans from the banks which also create book credits.

There is nothing alarming in this conclusion, though people who have been accustomed to regard bank deposits as so much cash paid in are sometimes startled when the other side of the matter is put to them, and to feel that banking credit is a kind of questionable conspiracy between banks and their customers. A little reflection shows that it is a beautiful piece of evenly working mechanism, by which coin is economized and a perfect currency is provided with extraordinary ease and cheapness. Nor need any sense of disillusionment be felt when it is realized that bank deposits, in so far as they are borrowed, are evidences of indebtedness quite as much as of wealth.

Everybody knows that in all long-established, well-ordered and industrious communities vast stores of wealth are accumulated; and even if they could be heaped up in banks and expressed in figures nothing would be gained by the information. But the contemplation of this mass of indebtedness, and of the cheque currency with which it is passed from hand to hand, is novel, stimulating and unique. It is a wondrous example of human ingenuity applied to the cheapening and furtherance of trade, finance and speculation. There is nothing quite like it anywhere else, and its development has only been rendered possible by the confidence, based on solid experience, of the majority of Englishmen in one another's commercial probity, and readiness to carry out a contract at all costs.

The only defect in the system is its perfection.

English banking has been so ably and successfully conducted, and has moved forward so steadily, especially since the foundation of the great joint-stock banks and the publicity which their establishment made necessary, that it sometimes becomes difficult to realize that banking is not merely a matter of quickening the wheels of commerce with a plentiful supply of credit when trade is prosperous, restricting credit when it outgrows its cash basis, writing off a few bad debts occasionally, and, year in and year out, making splendid profits by lending people the right to draw cheques, on the assumption that nearly all the cheques so drawn will be cancelled against one another, and will never involve a demand on the banks for legal tender cash. To the modern generation of bankers, to whom such a thing as a run on an English bank is a matter of tradition, a mere echo of a bad old past which is gone for ever, banking is sometimes a little apt to present itself as the simple process described above. But the thoughtful bankers, that is the great majority of the wary, cool-headed men who carry on this curious and magical business of providing currency and credit on a basis of mutual indebtedness between themselves and their customers, know well enough that there is another side to the question. Just as a man cycling through a crowded street depends, for his life, not only on his own skill but also on the care with which the rest of the traffic is driven, so the English banking system is dependent on the sanity and sense of the public as much as on its own soundness.

This dependence of the banks on the sanity and sense of the public arises out of the fact that bank deposits are payable in cash, either on demand, or in theory at a week's notice; and even the deposits at notice are practically liabilities on demand, because if any one who had money deposited at notice wanted it suddenly, a banker would find it very difficult to refuse to let him draw it. Hence it follows that if the public, or a considerable portion of it, became suddenly bereft of sense and sanity to a sufficient extent to make it want to take its money out all at once, the position of the banks would be uncomfortable, if they were not amply provided with coin and notes, and so able to quell the outbreak by meeting its first demands with a bold front.

It might appear that since bank deposits, as has been demonstrated, are largely created by credits given by way of loan or discount, any bank which happened to be subjected to the inconvenience of a run would only have to call in loans from its debtors to meet the demands of its depositors. But the matter could not really be settled by this simple method, in the first place because banks habitually make loans for fixed periods but have to meet liabilities, as we have seen, on demand; and, in the second, because in the case of a panic severe enough to cause a run on a bank, a large number of its debtors would almost certainly be obliged to admit their inability to repay their advances. The bank would find itself reduced to the unpleasant predicament of having to try to realize the securities or commodities, or other collateral, against which the loans had been granted, and in the state of panic which our hypothesis postulates would find it extremely difficult to do so, and would probably find it impossible to do so as rapidly as demands were pressed upon it.

Moreover, since we have already seen that the loans of one bank create the deposits of another, the attempt by one to call in its loans would inevitably cause pressure on the deposits of the others, and so the evil would swell and spread in a vicious circle. There is, however, no need to dwell on the possible horrors of a hypothetical banking panic. So much had to be said in order that the tremendous obligation might be realized which lies behind this business that is conducted so smoothly and easily, and that some appreciation might be gained of the responsibility that is faced by the affable and imperturbable gentlemen who conduct it. And it was also necessary to bring the skeleton out of the banking cupboard in order to emphasize the stern necessity for unceasing vigilance on the part of the banking world in the matter of its first weapon of defence against an outburst of public insanity which might start an importunate demand for cash from its bankers.

For in this matter the public and the banks act and react on one another, and the public is much less likely to be bitten with a mania for hoarding its money instead of leaving it in banks, if it knows that the banks are strong enough to meet a sudden demand without flinching. And hence it follows that, by keeping a strong line of defence in the shape of legal tender cash, the banks can do much to prevent the danger from arising, against which it is intended to protect them. Just as we saw that the note-issuing banks ran serious risks when they made advances in the form of their own notes without due regard to a store of metallic cash in which to meet their notes when presented, so the modern cheque-making banks have to keep an adequate proportion of legal tender cash against the right to draw cheques that they lend to their customers, or become liable to by other means.

If it were not for the fact that the credits which they lend represent the right to draw cheques payable on demand, the extent to which they could lend would be only limited by the demands of their customers, and the amount of security that their customers could provide. But this all-important fact makes the question of an adequate cash reserve against their liabilities an essential factor in the problem.

This reserve of cash consists of the gold and Bank of England notes that they have in their tills and in their vaults, and their balance at the Bank of England; it is the first line in the assets side of the balance-sheet, "cash in hand and at the Bank of England." On the other side, among the liabilities, we saw the entry "current, deposit and other accounts," and, if you work out the proportion of cash against those liabilities, you will see what is the proportion which the banks, whose position is there displayed, think it right and proper to keep.

There is no hard and fast rule on the point in England, and it would be absurd if there were, for the circumstances of banking business differ so widely, that what is a barely adequate proportion for one would be wastefully excessive for another. Good banking consists in giving as much assistance as possible to trade in the matter of credit, and at the same time restricting credit as soon as the proportion between cash and liabilities is below the point at which prudence and caution require that it should stand. This is the happy mean that the banker has to find. The exact point at which the mean stands is a matter which he is best able to judge; and though the desire to earn big dividends and the pressure of competition are strong incentives to him to place his ideal proportion too low, on the other hand the fine traditions of English banking and the wholesome dread of criticism, and of the moods of the multitude, are eloquent arguments in favour of wisdom and caution.

Good banking is produced, not by good laws, but by good bankers. Just as the most carefully planned constitution will inevitably break down if the men at the helm of government are incompetent or dishonest, so no skilfully devised banking system will make banking good, unless the banking is conducted by straight and able managers, or defend banking from suspicion by its customers, if other wheels in the financial machine have been proved to be unsound.

In the United States the national banks in the chief cities are compelled by law to keep a cash reserve equal to twenty-five per cent. of their deposits, and are liable to inspection by Government officers whose business it is to see that the cash is duly there. And yet, the panic of the autumn of 1907 saw the banks of the United States obliged to suspend payment because of mistrust on the part of the American public, which would have withdrawn most of its cash if the banks had not adopted the simple expedient of refusing to pay it. This mistrust was no doubt exaggerated, and in the case of most of the American banks was wholly unwarranted. But Americans, in discussing the matter, generally admit that it had a certain amount of basis in fact. The mere fact of legal regulation of the amount of cash probably makes the banks in America less careful with regard to the nature of the rest of their assets. Some of their managers are apt to think that, as long as they comply with the law, they have done all that is necessary, and so make inadvisable advances and hold unrealizable securities, perhaps because they are told to do so by some financial group that controls them.

There seems to be little doubt that the mistrust of the American public was to some extent due to a suspicion that its banks had been too closely connected with a great speculative campaign conducted on the New York Stock Exchange. But it also arose, perhaps chiefly, out of events over which the banks had no control, such as insurance scandals and revelations concerning the conduct of the Trusts, owing to which a general feeling of uneasiness concerning the whole financial position had been generated. Another cause, not of the panic but of the helplessness of American banking in the face of it, appears to have been the old-fashioned one of lack of cash, since the law concerning the cash proportions had been set aside by the creation of a large number of State banks and trust companies which did banking business, but were not amenable to the twenty-five per cent. law, and their weakness, in the eyes of indiscriminating depositors, infected the banks which had duly complied with the law, and multiplied the demands on them. This interesting side-light on the panic has been clearly displayed in an article by Mr. F. S. Mead, in the *Atlantic Monthly* of February, 1908.

In England, where the law imposes no rules on bankers in this matter, the public feels assured that its money is protected by the integrity and ability of those to whom it is entrusted. As long as this confidence lasts, all is well; but any one who trades on public confidence has not only to merit it, but also to provide for any accident that might arise if, in spite of his meriting it, the public were to withdraw it owing to some mistake on its part. Hence bankers have to be constantly alive to the necessity for keeping their position strong.

This they do, in the first place, by maintaining a high proportion of legal tender cash to liabilities. And legal tender cash means gold or Bank of England notes. And as Bank of England notes, above a certain number, can only be issued against gold, we come back once more to gold as the basis of credit.

Bankers' credit, as we have seen, consists of advances given to customers against goods or securities, and to that extent the goods and securities may be said to be the basis of credit. But since prudent banking demands that the extent of credits given must depend on the amount of the banks' legal tender cash, and that is gold or its equivalent, the amount of gold that is available in the hands of the banks, or of their bank, the Bank of England, is in some respects the most important influence on the supply of credit.

And now we are beginning to see why it is that so much importance is attached to the movements of gold to and fro across the Continents, and why an increase in the supply of gold in London makes discount rates easy and sends up the prices of securities, unless balanced by counteracting influences. Gold being the basis of credit, it obviously follows that, when there is more gold, credit will be more abundant, and that therefore bills will be discounted more cheaply, that is to say, the promise of money some day will fetch more money to-day; and that securities will go up in price, because money wherewith to buy them is to be had on more reasonable terms. But if counteracting influences, such as higher prices of commodities which necessitate a greater amount of credit for financing trade, are at work at the same moment, these effects of an increase in the amount of gold will be veiled. But they will be at work, and the increase of gold will be producing its effect, though it may not be detected on the surface.

Nevertheless, this dependence of the money market, and of the City as a whole, on the question of the amount of gold available is often a stumbling-block not only to the uninstructed public, but also to theoretical economists, who are apt to see in it a remnant of the Mercantile system. This system, with a view to keeping treasure in the country against an outbreak of war, endeavoured to regulate trade so that we might export more than we imported, creating a balance of exports, for which, it was hoped, the foreigner would pay in gold.

There is this much of resemblance between the two systems, that both the Mercantilist wanted, and the money market wants, to have a certain amount of gold in the country. The Mercantilist wanted it because, in days when the credit system had not been developed, war could only be financed with cash, a store of which was therefore desirable; and we saw in a former chapter that the Athenians achieved this object and glorified the Acropolis and their goddess by overlaying her statue with gold.* The only mistake made by the Mercantilists in this connection lay in the trade regulations that they made with a view to securing their object. The money market wants gold because gold is the only universally acceptable form of payment in times of panic, and is therefore needed as the bankers' reserve against accidents, and so regulates the supply of credit, because prudent bankers cannot give credit beyond a certain proportion to their holding of legal tender cash, gold or its equivalent.

And indeed, when we arrive at the conclusion

* p. 16.

that gold is the basis of credit, we are only restating the fact, which emerged in Chapter III., that all forms of cash are gold or representatives of gold, bank-notes being payable in gold if the holder demands it, and cheques being payable in gold or bank-notes. For since every credit involves a right to draw gold or notes, and notes are based on gold, it follows that credits cannot be given unless there is an adequate amount of gold in the hands of the banks which give them.

CHAPTER VI

LONDON THE WORLD'S MONETARY CLEARING HOUSE

So far money has been dealt with chiefly as a matter of internal experience, and from the point of view of the relations between the Englishman and his banker. In the account given of the origin and development of the bill of exchange the horizon was expanded for a time, but otherwise our attention has been concentrated on the forms of cash with which we English buy and sell commodities and services, and the process by which these forms of cash, and the right to draw and use them, are created by our bankers and their customers, through loans against goods and securities.

But the money market is a very much bigger and more interesting affair than it appears to be from this merely insular examination. It is, in fact, the most interesting of all markets, because it is world-wide to a greater extent than the market in anything else, with the possible exception of wheat.

The use of money in cash transactions is obviously world-wide; wherever men buy and sell they must use some medium of exchange which is commonly accepted in their country, even though it be only an inconvertible paper dollar printed at the caprice of a Central American Republic. But money in its wider sense, in the sense of bankers' credits, is also a matter of world-wide use, or at any rate demand, and it is only in London that money of this kind is to be had freely, and in the fullest meaning of its real definition, which implies, as we have seen, the right to demand, and the certainty of receiving, payment in gold.

It is clear that in order to be of any use in international finance, money must be immediately and unquestionably convertible into gold, the only form of payment which is universally and always acceptable in economically civilized countries. And money of this kind is only to be had in London.

In a pleasant American comedy produced very many years ago, one of the characters, holding out a bundle of papers to her husband, exclaims, "What's this? You said you'd give me some money!" "That's so," says the husband, "and so it is. Why, it's Wabash!" Wabash was the name of a railroad stock of somewhat problematical value, and quite useless as a medium of exchange for the purposes of household shopping. And any one who has a credit in any other centre but London, is liable to find himself, when he tries to realize it and turn it into cash, met by an offer of Wabash, or something equally inconvenient for his purposes.

The French are clever and versatile financiers, and the unfailing thrift which distinguishes the inhabitants of their country gives it a great and almost unsatiable power of absorbing investments, so that Paris is a very important factor in the international loan market. But the French temperament is essentially cautious, and the Bank of France does not attempt to do the business that we regard as banking, which includes readiness to meet all demands in gold. Its notes are convertible, but convertible at its option into either gold or silver; and it frequently takes advantage of this option, when it considers it undesirable to part with its gold. So that any one who has a credit in Paris has a credit which is of no international value, except in so far as he can make use of it, by means of the machinery of exchange, to buy a credit in London, which is convertible as a matter of course.

In theory Berlin has a gold standard, and the notes of the Imperial Bank are theoretically payable on demand in gold. But Germany is young as a financial nation, and its banks have been so busily and deeply engaged in promoting the industrial activities of the country that their resources and energies have been hitherto absorbed by this task, which they have performed with great success. Consequently they have not yet addressed themselves to this question of international banking and of being prepared to meet all demands on them in gold; and any one who wants to draw on the Imperial Bank's store to any large extent is likely to find obstacles and difficulties in his way, and is moreover likely to be met with a most discouraging countenance when next he requires accommodation. With the store of sagacity and scientific method that it has available, it is probable enough that Berlin may one day rise to the full responsibilities of a monetary centre, ready to face the real tasks of the international banker. At present, it is chiefly engaged with the solution of internal problems.

In New York the right to gold is less ostensible, but in ordinary circumstances more practicable. A credit in the United States carries with it the right to legal tender currency, and the general probability of securing what is called a gold certificate and turning it into the metal. But in the autumn of 1907, the whole American system broke down, and an interesting form of emergency currency, created to fill the gap caused by an outbreak of hoarding on the part of both the public and the banks, became the only available medium of exchange. It took the form of "clearing-house certificates" issued by the American banks, but whatever else they certified, it was not a certainty, or even a chance, of obtaining gold.

It is a cherished ambition among Americans to see New York some day established as the monetary centre of the universe, and with their vast natural resources and population there is no doubt that the United States can achieve any material tasks that they choose, if they can learn the necessary lessons and develop the necessary character. At present the characteristics of the typical American business man seem to fit him to do most things better than banking. His haste to grow rich, his eager enthusiasm and buoyant optimism followed by plunges into apprehension and depression, his quickness and versatility, his keen sensibilities, his craving for speculative excitement, and his genius in exaggeration—all these qualities make him an excellent producer, a first-rate distributor, a miraculous advertiser, an unapproachable gambler, and a somewhat questionable banker. There are hundreds of good bankers in the United States, who take a scientific interest in the problems of their business such as is comparatively rare among their English brethren. But they are developed in spite of their environment, and of the atmosphere of eager enterprise which makes it difficult to observe the humdrum laws and limitations of banking.

In 1907, the American banks were so strongly suspected by their own public of having made indiscreet use of their opportunities and capacities, that the public preferred to take care of its own money. And American banking met the situation by refusing to meet demands on it. Banks that can be so suspected by their own public, and can meet the suspicion in such a manner, have much to do and undo before they can constitute themselves into an international banking centre. Thoughtful Americans, from whose illuminating conversation I have gleaned these explanations of the shortcomings of American banking, also point out that it has not yet distinguished between solvency after an interval, and readiness to meet demands at once and without question. It seems, they say, to think that it has done all that can be expected if it holds securities that will ultimately, if it is given time, be capable of realization; and has not grasped the fact that no banker who takes a serious view of his banking responsibilities, could ask to be given time in meeting demands on him. The internal effects of the recent panic will doubtless soon be forgotten; but it will be long before international finance will look with much confidence on a draft on New York, which has been shown by experience to be inconvertible in times of crisis. When it has lived down this lapse, and provided the confidence that is now lacking, and the necessary machinery of a discount and money market, American banking may set about making New York the monetary centre of the world. And an American can learn anything, if he thinks it worth while.

Some of the smaller centres meet drafts on them in gold, but their limited resources limit their powers. Practical financiers of all nationalities will admit that a draft on another centre is only valuable from the international point of view from the readiness with which it can be turned, through the machinery of exchange, into a draft on London, which is the real cash of international commerce and finance, because money in the real sense of the word, gold or its equivalent, is only to be had, always and without question, and to any amount, in London. But this is only one of several reasons which make London pre-eminent as the money factory. Its money is not only more genuine, that is, more undoubtedly convertible than that of any other centre, but is also under normal circumstances both more cheaply and easily produced to suit the convenience of the user.

In recent years London has not been able to boast that its money is cheaper than that of all other centres; in the first place because the South African war destroyed a vast mass of English capital, and gave foreign countries, from which we bought material for it, claims on us which we have since then been painfully liquidating; and, in the second, because the great strain on the money machine caused by the extraordinary and world-wide activity of trade during the period which culminated in 1907, imposed on London, as the world's money factory, the necessity for guarding the basis of credit by the maintenance of high rates for money.

Perhaps it should here be explained that when

a large and increasing number of people require money, or the right to draw a cheque, for trade or other purposes, they naturally have to pay more for it, that is, they have to promise more money some day for the money here and now that they borrow. And the centre which alone is prepared to meet demands on it in gold is obliged to be especially careful to make them pay more, that is, to charge higher rates for money, so as to keep the demands on it within bounds, and also because, by charging higher rates, it attracts gold from abroad by a process which will be explained later.

But even though money was not always cheaper in London than elsewhere, it was always more easily to be had. In the case of the most obvious form of credit-raising, as for example when foreign governments are raising loans or American railroads are offering bond issues, there are times when France is a readier market for the borrower than England, owing to the greater thrift of the French people, which gives the Paris banks a bigger mass of accumulated capital to handle; but even then Paris often hands the borrower most of the money in the shape of a draft on London, and in times of uncertainty or strain London becomes the only place in which the loan-issuing machinery can work. In the summer of 1907 Japan wanted a loan to spend on the South Manchurian railway. It was a most inopportune request, for at that time the springs of capital had dried up under the stress of intensified drafts on them, and all the foreign lenders, who had previously competed for the privilege of supplying Japan's monetary needs, were deaf to the appeal. But London, having in former years prospered by reason of Japanese loans, found the money, with a bad grace, it is true, and amid protests against borrowing at a moment so ill chosen; but found it, at a time when in no other centre could such an operation have been contemplated.

This power is due to the unparallelled freedom and elasticity which mark the English system. It has been shown that bankers' money here merely means the right to draw a cheque, and is generally created by a banker lending it to a customer, who passes it on to a creditor, who pays it into another bank, and so one bank's loan becomes another bank's deposit. This system could be continued indefinitely if bankers were reckless, for the only checks on the multiplication of bankers' money are the supply of unpledged security, concerning the fitness of which as collateral the banker decides, and the relation that the banker thinks it right to maintain between liabilities and cash assets. And when the supply of ordinary bankers' money runs dry, borrowers have, as we shall see in a later chapter, another source to tap in the Bank of England, which again can lend as freely as it pleases, for in its case its loans probably become its own deposits, and the only restraint imposed upon it also is discretionary regard for the proportion between its cash and liabilities.

Now this elasticity is found nowhere else. In New York bankers have to keep their compulsory 25 per cent. of cash to liabilities, and the multiplication of credits, which create liabilities, is thus restricted by law. And the legal tender currency of the United States is peculiarly inelastic, though efforts are now being made to correct this defect. In Paris the amount of the note circulation of the Bank of France is limited by law, and the credit facilities available are limited by French caution and fear of taking risks. In Berlin complete elasticity exists in theory, and this theoretical elasticity of the German system is sometimes held up as a model for imitation in England, by reformers who fix their attention on the regulations in the two countries relative to the issue of bank-notes. In this respect Germany can certainly claim greater freedom. In England, as we have seen, after a fixed limit has been passed, not a note can be issued unless backed by gold; in Germany, also, there is a limit on the number of notes that may be issued against securities, but it may be passed at any time on payment of a tax of 5 per cent. interest on the further issue, and consequently when borrowers are prepared to pay more than 5 per cent. to the

Reichsbank, it can manufacture notes for them as rapidly as it considers to be prudent.

The elasticity of the German system thus only arrives when money is at a high price, and in England elasticity is constant and chronic, since the supply of currency here does not depend on the number of notes issued, but on the power of the community to draw cheques which is furnished to it by its bankers without any legal restriction, and subject only to the limits imposed by the prudence of the bankers, and the supply of unpledged security. The German system is very scientific and excellent on paper, for a banking-machine which is at the note-issuing stage of development. Under it notes can always be had at a price, and the high price involved reduces their volume when they are no longer needed. But we have seen that, at present, the preoccupation of German banking with the task of financing industrial development imposes restrictions on its other activities; and hitherto the elasticity of its currency arrangements has been hindered, for international purposes, by the fact that the currency created is not, in practice, to be relied on as completely and unquestionably convertible. The success with which Germany has faced and dealt with other problems makes it highly probable that this one of international banking will be faced by it and dealt with in due course.

But at present it leaves the responsibility to London.

The frequent assertion that money and a money market in the full sense of the words are only to be found in London, is not made by way of vainglorious boasting of English supremacy in this respect—rather, as will be seen later, because the very fact carries with it a danger and a responsibility that must on no account be lost sight of in any examination of London's monetary position. I am not attempting to deduce, from the unquestionable fact that London is the only monetary centre that is always ready to undertake the full responsibilities of international banking, that Englishmen are naturally abler and more trustworthy bankers and financiers than any other nation. There is much to be said for this contention, and both the virtues and defects of the English character help it to produce good bankers. But it must be admitted that English bankers have had the advantage of longer and less interrupted experience, and that exceptional circumstances have enabled them to make full and profitable use of it. At present, however, we are dealing with the facts of the present day and their consequences rather than their causes.

Quick-witted foreigners were very ready to see the advantages which London's credit system provided for them. "Lo!" they said, "here is a banker who has the courage to be prepared at all times to pay demands on him in gold, and the good luck or some other quality which enables him to do so. Moreover, he has a delightfully simple system by which any one who borrows from him becomes his creditor. Let us go and get a credit in London." So they brought their securities and borrowed on them, or brought their bills and discounted them, and so raised credits here, which they were enabled to count in their balance-sheets as so much gold in hand. And all this suited London very well, because London, being a banker and not a philanthropist, always charged its foreign—or any other —customers rather more for the loans and discounts than it allowed them for the credits so created, and also made various commissions and profits out of the process. And the foreigners, having begun the system of depending on London as a banking reserve centre, found it convenient to continue, and many of them decided that it was not safe to keep credits here which were only produced by borrowing, and that they ought to have more real balances in London which were really their own; and so they sent over goods or securities to be sold here, and left the money in London as a gold reserve. And this again suited London's convenience very well, for it took the goods and securities in exchange for its promise to pay, and now has the use of its customers' money to lend to other people. Which it does with easy freedom and profit to itself, and is enabled to continue to earn and expand this very comfortable income by merely being prepared to meet demands in gold, when called upon. This may seem to be rather an easy mode of earning a living, but the responsibility is, in fact, so great that no other centre tries to do business on the same lines.

But lest it should be thought that this account of the relations between London and her foreign customers is a creation of a bombastic fancy of a patriotically biassed Briton, let me quote an American opinion.

In 1901 a meeting of the American Bankers' Association was held at Milwaukee, and a paper was read by Mr. A. B. Stickney on the "Medium of Exchange and the Banking Function." In the course of this discourse he made the following remarks:—

"England has so organized her capital by means of her magnificent banking system that she is the banker of the world, and collects tribute from all the nations of the world in the form of interest, not for the use of her wealth or capital, but for the use of her credit. Paradoxical as it may sound, it is literally true that by means of her splendid banking organization England collects interest upon millions and millions of her own indebtedness to other nations. It is a very profitable business to collect interest on what one owes, and it is this which makes England the creditor nation."

The same interesting paper, which is printed together with many other thoughtful and illuminating utterances by practical American financiers, in a book called "Practical Problems in Banking and Currency," throws some light on the vexed question of the divergent interests of English trade and English finance, which make some English traders hostile to the international banking business done by their bankers. Mr. Stickney tells them that "the wares of commerce follow the drafts of commerce," in other words that the unrivalled international trade done by this little island is partly due to its unrivalled banking system. "I venture to suggest," he says to his American audience, "that you may subsidize ships to sail the seas, and your armies and navies may carry the flag to all the islands of the seas, but you will never control the commerce of the world, nor the wealth of the world, nor the world itself, until you have a banking system which can manage the exchanges of the world during commercial crises, and maintain at all times a fairly uniform rate of interest."

As to the maintenance of a fairly uniform rate of interest, London cannot compete with Paris. Paris, thanks to the protection given to the Bank of France by its right to meet demands in silver if it choose to do so, maintains a level of uniformity to which English traders, harassed by the greater fluctuations of Threadneedle Street, sometimes point with envy. But it is fair to remind English manufacturers that the big profits earned by London's international banking are a strong argument in favour of its advantage to the community as a whole, and that, even from their own point of view, it may be questioned whether the serene tranquillity of rates in France would not be readily exchanged by their French brethren and competitors for the ease and elasticity of credit operations as conducted here.

The business of managing the exchanges of the world during commercial crises is obviously thrown upon London, as things are at present, by its position as the only monetary centre which is prepared to produce gold on demand. In the autumn of 1907, when sudden crisis compelled the United States to liquidate their financial position, they ceased to a great extent from buying other people's goods, and began to sell everything in the shape of securities and commodities that they could dispose of, and, being a very rich and resourceful nation, held the civilized world in fee for the time being, demanding payment in gold.

Nearly all the gold shipped to New York at that time, estimated to have amounted to some twenty-five millions sterling, came from London.

But London, or the Bank of England, which, as usual at times of crisis, took a firm hold of London's operations, decided very early in the proceedings that it was not prepared to finance America's demands out of its own bullion-vaults. And so it raised its rate for money, and thus, by setting in motion a process, the working of which will be explained in a later chapter, pulled in gold from other centres to such an extent that some four-fifths of the amount shipped to the United States were supplied by foreign contributions.

It was, to all appearance, a very remarkable demonstration of London's complete control over the world's exchanges, and an interesting feature of the operation was the fact that Paris and Berlin, though obliged from motives of self-protection to let some of their gold go to assuage the American craving for it, did not send it direct to New York, but to London. Because they knew that gold that went to London could be got back again after a reasonable interval, but the state of affairs then prevalent in America made them very uncertain concerning the time that might elapse before the monetary arrangements of the United States could return to normal conditions.

It was thus shown, by the events of this memorable crisis, that London's tremendous responsibility of providing gold when it is required anywhere by a pressing emergency, is one that can be bravely and cheerfully borne as long as England is in a position, by applying sufficient twists of the monetary screw, to force other nations to contribute their share to the common necessity. And on the face of the matter it would appear that London's power to do so was demonstrated in a very unmistakable manner. Regarded superficially, the events of 1907 seemed to show that the Bank of England's rate has only to go up to a certain point, and the Bank Court need only to show a sufficiently stiff-necked determination to put it still higher if necessary, for gold to pour in from other centres.

Nevertheless, it must not be forgotten that the great producing power of the United States was a potent assistance to London in this particular case. We have seen that the Americans left off buying other people's goods and sold everything they could sell, so making the rest of the world their debtor for the time being. And it is an open question as to how much of the gold that was drawn into London, and so on to New York, came because it was owed to New York, and how much was drained out of other centres by London's masterful policy.

In most economic questions, these insoluble problems lie under the surface, and it is because it is so easy to miss them, and to ignore, or be ignorant of, their presence, that many people find it easy to be quaintly dogmatic about economic matters, which, in fact, become more and more complicated and obscure, the more thoroughly they are understood.

But whatever doubt there may be as to the causes of the ease and success with which London carried through its task of managing the world's exchanges during the latest crisis, there is no doubt whatever that the task lay upon London, owing to its position as custodian of the only gold reserve which is available at all times to all comers.

And hence emerges the consideration that English banking, which we have already seen to depend on the sense and sanity of the public at home, is also liable to pressure and disturbance if the public anywhere in the world, in any centre in which economic development has made considerable progress, takes it into its head to mistrust the custodians of its money.

And this consideration opens up a wide field. Sense and sanity in money matters may be expected with a fair approach to confidence in the British public, and also in the public elsewhere. But elsewhere, in countries where banking is less soundly conducted, the public may at times, without any loss of its sense or sanity, find genuine cause to mistrust its bankers. The mistrust of its bankers shown by the American public in 1907 was probably misplaced, as far as most of the banks were concerned; but it arose largely from suspicion of the trust companies, which conducted banking business on questionable lines, and were suspected not without reason. Between the well-conducted banks and the ill-conducted trust companies, the American public, recognizing no distinction, could not be expected to discriminate. The strength of a chain is that of the weakest link, and the reputation of the banks of any country in the eyes of the uninformed public is, in times of difficulty and mistrust, that of the least ably managed.

This complication, to which the leading and most prudent English bankers are very keenly alive, accounts for the energy with which they try to impress on their more backward brethren the duty of maintaining a high ideal of strength and caution. The latter are rather apt to resent what they regard as unwarranted and officious good advice from folk who, in their view, would do better to mind their own business. But banking in all countries hangs together so closely, that the strength of the best may easily be menaced if scandal arises owing to the mistakes of the worst.

But at present we are concerned with the foreigner; since it has been shown that banking trouble in other countries is almost bound to throw strain on London, and that in other countries banking trouble may sometimes arise from bad banking, we begin to see how many possibilities have to be guarded against by the London money market, and with how many thousand eyes and ears and with how acute telepathic perception it has to watch the signs of financial weather. We saw, in examining the relations of the banks with their home customers, that the perfection of the system and the absolute smoothness of its working, sometimes produce its one defect, in the shape of an inability on the part of some few unimaginative bankers to see reason for counsels of austere prudence. And in the relations of the English money market with its foreign customers we find the same thing. The system is so perfect and elastic and easy, and works so freely and prettily, that at times it runs the risk of working just a little too well.

When Falstaff was ordered on active service again, immediately after his Shrewsbury exploits, he complained that "it was always yet the trick of our English nation, if they have a good thing, to make it too common." Our English nation has a good thing in a credit system of marvellous elasticity. Clever foreigners appreciate the beauties of it very fully and are always ready to make eager use of it, raising credits here by means of finance paper or other devices, and sometimes it happens that we "make it too common." At the time of the latest crisis, the London market was very well prepared for possible trouble, because it had recently suffered from a fit of virtuous self-examination on the subject of the kind of paper that it was prepared to handle, and the number of finance bills current had been drastically reduced. But this is a matter which requires constant vigilance. It is not good business for the London market to give credits, too readily and too cheaply, against securities that could not easily be realized, to customers whose demands for cash are likely to be at any moment inconvenient. The problem of gold reserves, of which we hear so much from time to time, is only one side of a very big and many-sided question; another side is the necessity for holding only the most readily realizable assets, and yet another is the need for vigilance, common sense and promptitude in the regulation of the price of bankers' money. The double responsibility that the English money market has to face, of providing credit and currency for its home customers, and of meeting drafts on London from all parts of the world, in gold on demand, makes its functions doubly interesting. And these functions will be most simply set forth by means of a description of the various members which compose its body.

The chief and most important members of the London money market are the banks, bill-brokers and discount houses, accepting houses and foreign bankers, all of which are clustered round the central figure, the Bank of England. Their mutual relations and duties, and the manner in which the Bank of England regulates the action of the rest, can only be understood when we have seen with what class of work each of them is busied.

CHAPTER VII

THE CHEQUE-PAYING BANKS

We have now considered the various forms of cash money, and the process of the manufacture of the money, or right to draw a cheque, which is dealt in by lenders and borrowers in the money market. And we have seen that the right to draw a cheque in England carries with it the immediate and invariable right to demand gold, and so makes London the monetary centre of the world, since elsewhere this free convertibility of the currency of the country is not to be relied on with the same certainty. The tremendous responsibility undertaken by the London money market is thus apparent, and we have now to examine the various wheels of the great machine by means of which it carries on business.

In our chapter on the manufacture of money we formed a distant acquaintance with the greatest of these wheels, when we saw that the cheque currency of England is manufactured by the banks, largely through the loans and discounts by means of which they create deposits which represent mutual indebtedness between them and their customers.

The provision of currency has thus passed into the hands of the other banks, and the Bank of England's note issue is chiefly used as a basis of the cheque currency which they provide, that is, is held in reserve by them to meet cheques that may be presented for payment in legal tender cash—notes or gold. Before we go further, however, we must make sure of what we mean when we talk or write about the banks. I have headed this chapter "Cheque-paying Banks," manufacturing a very ugly phrase in the hope that it may be clear. For it may be said that the essential function of English banking, which differentiates it from other institutions which are very nearly but not quite banks, is this fact that it gives its customers the right to draw cheques against credits arising sometimes from the deposit of cash, more often from advances against security or the discounting of bills, and is prepared to meet these cheques on presentation by paying coin or notes across the counter. The phrase cannot claim the watertight completeness of a logical definition, but it is roughly descriptive. It includes the country banks, which in their turn bank with the London banks. The cheque-paying banks, in short, for the purposes of this inquiry must be taken to include the native banks of this country, with the exception of the Bank of England, which may be regarded either as the foundation of the banking edifice or as a pinnacle on its summit, but in any case stands by itself. But they do not include the merchant firms and accepting houses, who do a business which is often described as banking, but do not meet cheques drawn on them with legal tender cash, but with a cheque drawn on one of the banks which we classify as cheque paying.

It need not be said that banking groped its way to its present perfection through many difficulties and mistakes. A Royal Commission which inquired into the subject in the early part of the nineteenth century laid bare the fact that in 1793 more than a hundred English county banks failed, and that in 1810 to 1817 six hundred closed their doors. Novelists of earlier generations made effective use of bad banking in the plots of their novels, and actual fact was even more romantic than fiction in the days when the speed of a post-chaise full of bullion might save a bank which was troubled by a run, and difficulties of transport were increased by the highwaymen who infested the roads. In 1793 "a general panic was raging in London; many bankers failed, some of whom acted for their northern brethren. Fresh London agents had to be appointed and duly advertised in the local papers. This helped to spread alarm. Every holder of a note was anxious to convert it into gold. Scores of country bankers were in London, trying, by any means, to gather the precious metal, with which, when obtained, they immediately posted home, disregarding the perils of robbery on the road. The very bank that had reported 'all quiet and undisturbed' on the 20th had before the close of the month (March) first a clerk and then two partners in London seeking gold, a supply of which they obtained and carried north with all speed. Mr. Rowland Burdon, partner in the Exchange Bank, Newcastle, was in the metropolis upon the same mission. On the return journey his post-chaise was stopped by footpads, who pinioned the banker and rifled his pockets. The bullion fortunately escaped their notice." *

It is recorded in the interesting work just quoted that the great banking family of Backhouse of Darlington were wont, when they found it necessary to replenish their gold store and were anxious to avoid the suspicions that would be aroused if they were known to be doing so, to drive quietly off in a gig as if about to visit a local meeting and to change into a post-chaise and four at Scotch Corner, a noted place on the North Road. The practice throws an interesting light on the extreme care which had to be exercised by bankers in early days in order to do nothing which could possibly excite suspicion. And having mentioned the Backhouse family I cannot avoid the well-known story

* Maberly Phillips, "History of Banks, Bankers and Banking."

of the attempt made, according to legend, by Lord Darlington early in the nineteenth century deliberately to break their bank. It is stated that he actually instructed his tenants to pay him their rents in Backhouse notes, meaning when he acquired a sufficient number of them to present them all at once, demand gold, and so make the bank put up its shutters. Jonathan Backhouse was apprised of this intention, and went off to London post-haste for the necessary supply of gold. On his way back one of the fore-wheels came off the chaise, and rather than wait to have the wheel replaced the banker piled the gold at the back part of the chaise, so "balancing the cash" and driving into Darlington upon three wheels. "By this sudden *coup* the bank was so well provided with specie that when Lord Darlington's agent presented a very large parcel of notes they were all promptly cashed, the Quaker quietly remarking, 'Now tell thy master that if he will sell Raby, I will pay for it with the same metal.'" *

Finally, I must risk still further the charge of irrelevant anecdotage by telling the story of the man who came down the steps of his bank, the door of which had been closed against him, stumbled under the shock of his ruin into the arms of a friend, and apologized by saying, "The fact is, I had lost my balance."

* Ibid.

It would be pleasant to linger over the romance and humours of the primitive days of banking, but it is perhaps still pleasanter, and certainly more profitable, to record that both the comic and tragic side of bank failures, as a common experience, are to the present generation only a matter of tradition. And yet they are not really a matter of very ancient history, and I have talked with a grey-haired manager of a country bank, now absorbed into a great joint-stock concern, who was behind his counter during a run and asked a customer who came in to draw his balance how he would take it, and was astonished by being asked for the bank's own notes.

The improvement in English banking has been coincident with the development of joint-stock banking, a fact which is the more interesting because it was noted by keen-eyed Adam Smith that the joint-stock system is particularly well suited to banking. His reasons are worth quoting. "Though," he says, "the principles of the banking trade may appear somewhat abstruse, the practice is capable of being reduced to strict rules. To depart upon any occasion from these rules, in consequence of some flattering speculation of extraordinary gain, is almost always extremely dangerous, and frequently fatal to the banking company which attempts it. But the constitution of joint-stock companies renders them in general more tenacious of established rules than any private co-partnery. Such companies, therefore, seem extremely well fitted for this trade." *

Apart from this regular working by rule and tradition, joint-stock companies have for some time been subjected to greater publicity than private firms. When there is a large body of shareholders, it is impossible to maintain the same dignified secrecy and reserve concerning the position of a business, which is generally observed by private enterprises: and any bank which has to issue a statement of its position is bound to issue a strong one, or it would at once be the subject of cavil and suspicion, which might have unfortunate results. Hence it is that publicity has compelled the banks to keep themselves strong, in wholesome fear of the criticism of their rivals and of other members of the monetary body. A good balance-sheet was soon seen to pay those who produced and published it, and the banks found that by giving publicity to their position they gained and maintained public confidence: so much so that nearly all the private banks, though not bound to do so by law, now publish annual or half-yearly balance-sheets.

Publicity has thus done much for banking, and its good effects are generally recognized by the most enlightened bankers of to-day, some of whom are strong advocates for its extension. The regular

* "Wealth of Nations," book v., chapter 1.

publication of half-yearly balance-sheets was a great step forward. But much may happen between January 1 and June 30, and again between July 1 and New Year's Eve, and the freedom and facility with which the English system of banking works is a temptation to bankers to employ too freely the admirable machinery with which they supply credit and currency to the commercial and financial community, and to build up too big a basis of credit on too small a foundation of cash. The fact that their doing so facilitates trade and finance and quickens the wheels of commerce all the more efficiently, as long as no untoward result follows, makes it difficult to advocate reform without affecting the interests of a large and powerful multitude, and also necessitates the greatest care in dealing with a very delicate and difficult subject. Nevertheless, it must be remembered that trade and speculation that are based on inflated credit and inadequately secured currency carry with them dangers that are unpleasant to contemplate even in imagination, and it may also be contended that the strength of the resistance to the more frequent application of publicity to the position of the banks is in itself a sufficient evidence of the urgent necessity of the reform.

It has long been recognized that it is the duty of currency-creating banks to issue frequent statements of their position. The Bank of England has published a weekly account regularly ever since the Act of 1844; the Bank of France does the same, and so do all the chief Continental banks of issue. And in New York, where there is no central bank, there is a weekly statement of the position of the Associated Banks. It may be contended that since the Bank of England makes this weekly statement, and is the keeper of the ultimate reserve of the country, all that is necessary is already done, and that English banking is in this respect quite as subject to publicity as its Continental counterpart. But the conditions in England are wholly different, for, as we have seen, the development of the use of cheques in England has reduced the position of the Bank of England's note issue to one of quite secondary importance as currency, and has made the banks on which the cheques are drawn, the chief creators of currency for this country. The publication of the Bank of England's weekly account shows how much gold it has, and how many notes it has issued against it, but tells us nothing as to how much credit the other banks have built up on the basis of this gold and these notes.

After the crisis of 1890, which was faced with most satisfactory equanimity by the English banks, the late Lord Goschen urged on the bankers the desirability of a higher proportion of cash reserves, and, doubtless observing that in order to maintain a continually higher standard, more frequent publicity was essential, asked for monthly statements. His suggestion was immediately adopted by most of the principal London banks. This was something gained, but the partial nature of the reform robbed it of much of its advantage, and attached to it obvious evils and unfairness. None of the private banks followed Lord Goschen's hint, and one of the greatest of them, which has since joint-stocked itself in conjunction with a large number of other private firms, still remains outside the circle of monthly publishers of statements. And none of the country banks, with which the country branches of the London banks are in continual competition in one place or another, considered that Lord Goschen's admonition in any way concerned them.

The bankers who had followed it were thus placed at a disadvantage, if it be a disadvantage to have an incentive applied to them in the direction of prudent banking. And it must be admitted that from the point of view of earning dividends and obliging customers, that banker is temporarily favoured who has least inducement to restrict his credits according to the dimensions of his cash, though ultimately he runs all the greater risk of being a danger to himself and to the rest of the community.

Certainly the banks which do publish monthly statements of their position appear to regard the fact as a handicap to which their competitors are not subjected, and the reluctance of the latter to join the movement is presumptive evidence in favour of the view that they make an unfair use of their comparative freedom from publicity. If this be so, there is clearly all the more reason why publicity should be applied to them.

Moreover, it has become evident that even monthly statements are insufficient if they are to show the position on one day only, the day on which the statement is made out, and are not to give some evidence of the relation between the banks' cash and liabilities throughout the period covered. A periodical "tightness of money," as Lombard Street calls it, towards the end of every month, when the monthly statements of the publishing banks are being prepared, leads irresistibly to the conclusion that some of them call in loans or diminish discounts, and so increase their cash holding in order to make their position stronger on the day of its publication. One of them, the London and County, in order to show that it at least is no party to this system of publishing misleading statements, adopted early in 1908 the practice of giving the amount of its daily average cash holding throughout the month, and has thus led the way towards the abolition of a practice which is obviously quite unworthy of the high traditions of English banking.

It might, perhaps, be unfair to expect all the banks to give a full statement of the daily average position of their cash and deposits, owing to the extra amount of clerical work involved, and an efficient alternative was advocated a few years ago by a distinguished chairman of the Bankers' Institute in the course of a presidential address, in which he suggested that all banks should publish a weekly statement.

The present system by which publicity is applied to banking, once a year in some cases, once a half-year in others, and once a month in others, is clearly illogical and unfair, and the fact that obstinate resistance is offered to publicity, especially by certain of the country banks, only shows how necessary is its application.

As will be seen later, the question is intimately connected with the wider problem of the collective gold reserve, and it has been insisted over and over again by practical and distinguished bankers that the proportion of cash to liabilities, in the case especially of some of the country banks, is inadequate, and that periodical publication of their position is an important step towards a remedy for this evil. All that is asked of the banks is that they should show what they are doing, and the reluctance of some of them to do so is not a favourable sign.

The fact that the great majority of the banks do give adequate attention to the relation between their cash and their liabilities rather increases the difficulties of the question, because it brings into being a school of thought which maintains, after the manner of Doctor Pangloss, that all is for the best in the best of all possible banking worlds, and resents any suggestion of improvement as an impertinent intrusion; but these optimists must remember that, if ever banking trouble should arise in this country, they must not expect the public to discriminate too nicely between the good banks and the less good, so that an indiscretion on the part of a weaker brother might cause serious inconvenience to bankers of the most strait-laced virtue. But the more frequent publication of accounts is a matter which will inevitably be settled, and let us leave it with the hope that the next step will not, like the last, be taken by the banking world as the result of crisis.

It has already been stated that the great improvement in English banking, which has changed the picturesquely exciting system illustrated at the beginning of this chapter for one of monotonous solidity, has coincided with the development of banking by joint-stock companies. And it is interesting to note that the law of the land, as far as it could, presented an insuperable obstacle to this development. It gave a monopoly of joint-stock banking in London to the Bank of England, but it defined banking, as banking was when this monopoly was given, as the right to issue notes. But when the nature of banking changed, and it became the business of a banker not to give a customer a credit and let him take out notes, but to give a customer a credit and let him draw cheques, it was perceived that the Bank of England's monopoly did not prevent the establishment of joint-stock banks in London; and so the law, in spite of its manifest intention, was practically annulled by a change in banking practice which its framers could not possibly have been expected to foresee.

It was in 1834 that this discovery bore fruit in the foundation of the London and Westminster Bank, and since then it may be said that English banking has passed into the hands of the joint-stock banks by their rapid development, by the readiness with which they absorbed the old private banking firms, and finally by the action of a large number of the latter, which were amalgamated in 1896 into a great joint-stock bank, named Barclay and Company, after the principal firm among its components.

The distinguishing feature of the new banking which has thus grown up is the system of banking by branches. In former days each bank stood by itself with its customers all in one neighbourhood, and if it had branches they were quite few and confined within a comparatively small area. The new banking opens branches all over the country, or buys the interests of other banks, and seems to seek to diffuse its business as widely as possible. The consequence is that English banking, instead of consisting of a large number of small firms or companies providing monetary facilities each for its little band of customers, has been systematized into a compact army, composed of a few well-regulated and strongly equipped regiments, each of which has its companies and outposts scattered up and down a big area, but worked from a common centre, and with excellently organized arrangements by which the needs of each district can be watched over and provided for.

This development has great advantages, the most obvious of which is the imposing magnitude of the gigantic modern banks as compared with the pigmy firms of the old system of separate entities. Since the banker trades on public confidence, and size is the most impressive quality for striking the public imagination, the process of amalgamation and branch building has certainly strengthened banking in a most important respect. And it need hardly be said that it has also done a great work in regulating the ebb and flow of monetary facilities and providing a number of channels, all connected with the central reservoir, by which the process of financial irrigation can be most easily and cheaply conducted, and the supply can most readily be applied to any part that may happen to be suffering from drought. As long as all goes well in the world of banking the present system will readily be acknowledged to be a great improvement on its predecessor.

At the same time, it must not be forgotten that this multiplication of bank branches has also multiplied the number of points at which the banking body is vulnerable, and that, if it should so happen that all did not go quite well in the banking world, and every branch open became a sucker instead of a feeder, the magnitude of the defenders' task would be greatly increased by the diversity of the outlets for the banks' life-blood. A cash reserve which would be adequate enough for an institution which keeps all its liabilities under one roof may easily be meagre for one which has smaller liabilities scattered over different points in a score of counties.

From this point of view the size of a bank, which is so striking an indication of solidity in the eyes of the uninstructed, presents a different aspect on closer examination. For it is usual to measure the size of a bank by its deposits, in other words by its liabilities, and by the number of its branches. And when the liabilities are not only great but widespread, they become still more misleading as a test of greatness. In estimating the wealth of an individual we should hardly begin by enumerating the number of millions that he owed, and the number of places in which he owed them. We should admire the magnitude of his credit operations, but in assessing his solidity we should most of all want to know how liquid were the assets which he held against this mass of debt. And so with banks. The bigger they are, and the more widely scattered their places of business, the greater is their need for prudence and foresight. It need not be said that these platitudes are fully recognized by those in charge of the many-branched banks.

We have seen that the banks, by creating the cheque currency with which English commerce and finance is now conducted, play a supremely important and responsible part in the domestic economy of the London money market. But this is only one side of their importance. They also, in normal times, that is, at times in which it is not necessary for the Bank of England to intervene and control the position, regulate the price of money in London as indicated by the rate for day-to-day loans and short fixtures, and the discount rates for bills of all dates. To a certain very limited extent, it is true, they are controlled or affected at all times—or at nearly all times—by the Bank of England's official rate, because the allowance that they make to depositors for the use of their money is generally —though not invariably—1½ per cent. below Bank rate. But, besides the funds which they hold on deposit, they also have very large sums left with them on current account,* on which they in most cases pay no interest at all, so that it often happens that they can and do lend in the money market at a lower rate than they pay to depositors. And the price at which they lend in the money market makes the market rate for loans, except on quite rare occasions.

It seems to be impossible to go straight forward in this inquiry, and now we must pause and explain the meaning of this phrase, the market rate for loans. If I may be allowed to express it with a view to clearness and simplicity rather than fulness and precision, it means the rate at which the banks are prepared to lend money—or the right to draw a cheque—to the bill-brokers. The bill-brokers ought to be explained too, but they must wait for the next chapter, and in the meantime can be described roughly as specialists who devote themselves to discounting bills, or acting as intermediaries in the discounting of bills. If you look at the aggregate bank balance-sheet drawn up to illustrate our chapter on the manufacture of money, you will see on the right-hand side among

* The only banks which at present separate current from deposit accounts in their balance-sheets are—The Union of London and Smith's Bank, Messrs. Glyn, Mills, Currie & Co., and Messrs. Hoare. On June 30, 1908, the Union owed £24,204,000 on current account, and £11,812,000 on deposit account, the former being thus rather more than double the latter. At the same date Glyn's current accounts were £10,009,738, and their deposit accounts £4,289,486. On July 6, Messrs. Hoare showed current accounts £1,885,819, and deposit accounts £561,519.

the assets first the cash in hand and at the Bank of England, the bank's first line of defence, and then "loans at call or short notice."* These loans are made day by day by the banks to the bill-brokers, money lent to whom is regarded by bankers as a second line of defence, since it is habitually placed either "at call" from day to day or for periods which do not usually exceed a week; and can thus, in theory at least, be called in readily. The phrase also, in some cases, covers loans from banks to stock-brokers; but when the rate for money is quoted in the City, it usually means the rate between banks and bill brokers. And any one who reads the opening paragraph of a newspaper money article and is puzzled to find that there was very little demand for money, and day-to-day loans were easily to be had for some apparently absurdly unremunerative rate, need not therefore infer—as sometimes happens—that a great revolution has been effected in human nature, and that money is no longer an object of man's ambition. The phrase generally misleads those who are not used to City jargon, and I once heard an indignant gentleman in a railway carriage vehemently asserting that the newspapers talked infernal nonsense, because he had apparently strayed by some mistake into the money article of the one that he had been reading, and had learnt from it that money was "unuseable," and that

* p. 59.

balances had been offered in vain at 1 per cent. It appeared that he had spent the previous day in a fruitless endeavour to induce his bank to allow him an overdraft on the security of certain pictures, apparently his own works, and of quite problematical value; he had offered to give up to 10 per cent. for the accommodation, and was so deeply stirred by the statement that there was no demand for money at 1 per cent. that he roundly dismissed all City journalists as unfit even to be art critics, which appeared to be the extreme limit of condemnation in his opinion.

It is very important that the meaning of the word "money" as used in the City should be clearly grasped, for we shall find that the rate for this money and the facilities for getting it are most important wheels in the machine, and it is essential to keep a tight hold of the correct significance of the phrase.

Money, then, has a special sense when spoken of by the chief dealers in it, thus presenting yet another example of the confusing inconsistencies of economic nomenclature. In this sense it is usually a loan granted by a banker to a bill-broker for a day or for a period not exceeding a week. The rate for this class of accommodation thus represents the price of the right to draw a cheque given to a borrower of the highest possible credit against securities of the highest possible class, and for the shortest possible period. And it is thus quite misleading to draw any inference from it concerning the rate that ought to be paid under different conditions.

This rate is, in normal times, practically decided by the cheque-paying banks. Other lenders, such as the Indian Government's representatives, or the finance houses or merchants, sometimes have large balances employed among the bill-brokers, but the deciding voice concerning the value of the rate for short loans is ultimately that of the banks. And it is in the extreme elasticity of this rate that we begin to detect the great difficulties that have to be coped with by those who control the London money market. I must be allowed for the moment to beg the question that the London money market has to be controlled, and to add that many of the difficulties of London's position arise from the fact that many members of the money market do not adequately recognize that it has to be controlled, and that even those who do waver constantly between the horns of a dilemma which is ever present, one being their own immediate interest, and the other that of the market as a whole and in the future.

For example, any given banker at any given moment may most reasonably consider that the rate at which he lends money to the bill-brokers is a question which merely concerns himself and his duty to his shareholders. He has so much cash, so much invested in securities, so much advanced to customers, and a further proportion which he can, according to the rules by which he regulates his business, lend to the bill-brokers at call or short notice. Any rate for this is better than none, and, if the bill-brokers only bid him 1½ per cent. for it, why should he not take it rather than lose the profit to be made by the creation of so much credit? If he does not, he will very probably cause the bill-brokers to go across the street and bid a rival bank 1¾ per cent., and the only result of his abstinence will be to swell the profits of a competitor. From the point of view of the individual banker these arguments are irrefutable. And yet it is much to be desired that some system could be devised of more harmonious agreement among bankers as a whole, by which the rate for money, in the City sense of the word, could be made less mercurial, and especially could be prevented from falling to a merely nominal level, and so, as we shall see, unduly depressing discount rates, encouraging all kinds of kite-flying and the production of finance paper, turning the foreign exchanges against London, and increasing the difficulties of those responsible for the maintenance of the gold reserve.

We have seen that the banks supply English commerce and finance with most of its currency, and also regulate the price of money in the money market. But we have not nearly exhausted their important functions. They also, in normal times, are chiefly responsible for regulating the discount rate in London, that is, the rate at which bills of exchange drawn, as described in a previous chapter, for payment at a future date, can be turned into immediate cash. This market rate of discount is an even more momentous matter than the market rate for money, because it has a very important bearing on the foreign exchanges, another of the complicated questions which have to be dealt with later on. The importance, in fact, of the market rate for money arises largely out of its effect on the market rate of discount; if the bill-brokers are supplied freely with money at low rates, and think that they see a probability of the continuance of this free and cheap supply of credit, they are naturally encouraged to discount bills at low rates, so that the banks which regulate the money rate thus exercise a strong and direct influence on the discount rate.

But they also exercise a still stronger and more direct one by being themselves large discounters of bills, so much so that many bill-brokers contend that it is the bankers who directly determine the market rate of discount. And this is probably true, for most of the bill-brokers are chiefly intermediaries, and only discount bills with the object and intention of promptly rediscounting the greater number of them; and the bankers are the chief buyers with whom they can most regularly count on placing the bills that they take; consequently, when it is known that two or three of the chief banks are not taking bills below, for example, 3 per cent., this fact has a marked effect on the market rate of discount, that is, the rate quoted by the bill-brokers. And as the market rate of discount is an important factor in influencing the foreign exchanges, which in turn are an important factor in influencing the inward and outward movements of gold, we come round once more to the great importance of the policy pursued by the banks with regard to discounting bills.

Still more important and delicate do their duties become when there arises any question of discriminating between the classes of bills that will be taken, whether the objection be to bills of a certain kind, or to bills drawn on a certain house. By merely intimating to the bill brokers that he does not want many * "house bills," or many bills drawn on a certain name, or that he is not taking paper which is too obviously of the kite-flying order, a bank manager can at any time profoundly affect the inner working of the financial machine. The exercise of such a power has to be handled with the nicest discretion, for any such intimation, especially when the paper of any particular accepting house is

* Page 52.

objected to, generally produces a good deal of gossip and conjecture, and is certain to have some effect on the credit of the firm that is indicated as having been accepting more heavily than its resources are considered to warrant.

And this part of the bankers' duty in watching over the volume of acceptances, and seeing that the accepting houses do not overstep the bounds of prudence, is complicated by the fact that the banks have themselves lately taken up the business of acceptance to a greatly increased extent. But this feature in their business will be more fitly discussed when we come to consider the position and function of the accepting houses as such.

Finally, the bankers fulfil a highly important function by providing credit facilities for Stock Exchange speculation. This they do both directly and indirectly. Directly by making loans to their customers on the security of stocks and shares which the latter buy, not as investments, but because they think they will rise in price, or will return a higher rate of interest than the rate which the banker will charge for the loan; and indirectly by making loans to members of the Stock Exchange which the latter employ in financing the speculative commitments of the public. The rates earned by bankers for this kind of accommodation are generally profitable, and the most strait-laced moralist would hardly question their right to provide credit for this purpose. In fact, in the case of direct loans to his ordinary customers, the banker need not necessarily know that the transaction is intended for speculation. Let us suppose that you arrange with your banker for an advance against a line of Argentine bonds, which you want to buy because you think you see a chance of reselling them at a profit, or because you can buy them to pay you 5 per cent., and you can get a loan from your banker at 3 per cent., and pocket the difference of 2 per cent. In such a case, as far as your banker knows, you may want the credit in order to buy a house, or to engage in some productive commercial operation. Nevertheless, in most cases he is probably in a position to make a fairly accurate guess, and when he is lending directly to members of the Stock Exchange, he knows well that in nine cases out of ten he is financing the purchase of securities by those who for one reason or another are not in a position to pay for them, and so is facilitating the speculative holding of stocks as opposed to the real possession of them by investors who have paid for them out of savings.

By performing this function, within due limits, the banker is carrying out a perfectly legitimate side of his business, and assisting operations which are beneficial to the community as a whole. The majority of speculators probably lose more money than they make, but if they choose to indulge in this expensive form of amusement, it is not their banker's business to interfere with it, and during the course of the process they are unconsciously rendering a financial service by promoting the freedom of markets and facilitating dealings in securities.

Nevertheless, the readiness with which bankers can place credit at the disposal of speculators sometimes has bad effects, which have to be watched for carefully by those who regulate the supply of it.

For example, there can be no doubt that it was an important cause, among others, of the abnormally high level to which the prices of well-secured stocks were forced in the period of exceptionally cheap money in 1896-97, when Consols touched 114, and "gilt-edged" securities could with difficulty be found to yield the buyer 2½ per cent. This state of things was a great hardship to the real investor, and was undoubtedly brought about to some extent by the number of enterprising folk who borrowed from their banks at 1 per cent. or so against gilt-edged securities yielding 2½ per cent., and pocketed the difference accruing from the yield on the stock and the profit arising from the advance in its price, which continued merrily up to a point. The demoralization of the gilt-edged market, dating from that golden period, and quickened by subsequent wars and other causes, is still being painfully lived down. But this is a point which perhaps does not directly concern the banker, as such, though as a large holder of securities he is affected by any tendencies which warp the true course of markets. Still, he is quite justified in arguing that he is not to blame if his customers, by the use that they make of the credit that he gives them, produce abnormal effects on prices.

More to the purpose is the fact that Stock Exchange securities are only to a limited extent liquid, that is to say, realizable at a moment's notice, and that the more a banker wanted to call in credit granted against them the less liquid they would be. It was once gravely contended by a gentleman who was opposed in principle to the existence of Government debts, that if every holder of Consols wanted to sell at once, and there were no buyers, the price would be *nil.* Which is one of those absurd truisms which contain their own refutation in their very truthfulness, but nevertheless are only caricatures, so grotesque as to be unrecognizable, of a very real fact. In this case the fact is the less exciting platitude that the more people there are who want to sell stock, and the fewer who want to buy it, the lower its price will be, and the less easy it will be to sell it at all. It is boasted that the market in Consols is so free that they can be sold on Sunday. And there are other securities enjoying the advantage of an international market, that is, of being freely dealt in in Paris and on the other Continental Bourses, which can really be disposed of at any time, at a price. But they are not many, and in times of difficulty or crisis, the possibility of which can never be wholly absent from the mind of a prudent banker, it is quite conceivable that securities, quoted officially at substantial prices, could not be turned into cash on any terms, and that the lending banker might find the credit that he had granted used to draw away his cash, without being able either to compel his customer to repay him or to convert the collateral and so replenish his resources.

From this it must not be inferred that bankers commit any indiscretion in conducting this class of business. All these matters are questions of degree, and if due attention be given to the class of security advanced against, and the extent to which these transactions are entertained, nothing can be said against them by a reasonably minded critic. As we have seen in a previous chapter, the finest class of security for a banker to hold or to finance is the bill of exchange drawn against real produce of universal consumption which is moving into the hands of those who will consume it, and so will pay for itself in due course. In all other securities the existence of a buyer to meet the views of the seller is more or less problematical. However intense the panic, the human race must be fed and clothed, but the extent to which it will take securities from those who want to sell them will vary in an inverse ratio to the severity of the panic. And though it would be absurd to argue from this ground that bankers ought to hold nothing but produce bills, it is quite relevant that the limits to the negotiability of some other securities should be constantly kept in view.

This chapter has grown to a portentous length, which must be excused owing to the great importance of its subject. "I am always willing to run some hazard of being tedious in order to be sure that I am perspicuous," said Adam Smith, and was fortunate in being able to write so confidently. I have to face the certainty of being tedious, and can only hope that I run some hazard of being perspicuous. What I have tried to make clear is the enormously important function of the cheque-paying banks in the English money market. Recapitulated in tabular form it may be expressed thus:—

By providing their customers with cheque-books they create the currency which settles the great majority of commercial and financial transactions and much of the retail traffic of daily life.

By discounting bills and making advances to bill-brokers and other customers they create the credits by which commerce and finance are carried on; and these credits become in turn their liabilities on current and deposit account.

They regulate, in normal times, the current rates for money in London.

They regulate, in normal times, the discount rates current in London, which have an important effect on the foreign exchanges, and so on the maintenance of London's gold reserve.

They are large acceptors of bills, and so, again, facilitate commerce and create instruments which are readily convertible into cash or credit.

By advancing to customers or stockbrokers against Stock Exchange securities they facilitate speculation, and thus to some extent affect the prices of stocks and shares.

It is a tremendous function, and it follows obviously that the cheque-paying banks are in the aggregate the most important members of the financial body. We shall find that, with one exception, the other members are more or less dependent on them, and can only work with the assistance of the credit created by them. The one exception is the Bank of England, which exercises special functions which will be more fully described hereafter, and in abnormal times regulates the whole course of the money market. But even it derives much of its power from the fact that it acts as banker to the cheque-paying banks.

CHAPTER VIII

THE BILL-BROKERS AND DISCOUNT HOUSES

We have seen that the main functions in the manufacture of credit and currency are performed by the cheque-paying banks, and we have now to examine the operations of several minor but important subsidiaries, which the specializing tendency of civilization has called into being.

The banks manufacture money by making advances, that is, giving the right to draw cheques, against all kinds of security and by buying or, according to the technical phrase, discounting bills, that is, giving the immediate right to draw a cheque or cash in return for an instrument which conveys the right to cash at a later date. The bill-brokers appear to have originally performed the function of intermediaries between the banks who were buyers of bills and the merchants who had bills to dispose of. This function they still carry on to a great extent, and, in so far as they remain bill-brokers, this is the chief part of their business. But several distinctions have arisen through the natural tendency to diversification of function, and it may now be said that there are roughly three classes of firms to be included under the titles which head this chapter.

(1) There is the bill-broker pure and simple, who devotes himself entirely to taking a parcel of bills from the merchants, accepting houses, foreign and colonial banks, and other chief agents, who receive them in batches by every mail, and selling them there and then on the best terms that he can obtain, receiving a commission for his pains, and for his knowledge of the market. This variety, which is the real survivor of the original bill-broker, is now comparatively rare. It is commonly described by the term "running broker."

(2) There is the retail dealer in bills, who is still generally called a bill-broker, but does not work on commission but buys bills outright, either from the running broker, or from the merchants and accepting houses, or from foreign correspondents, but nevertheless does not, as a rule, hold them himself until they mature, but sells them to the banks and other buyers, selecting the dates and classes of paper that the several buyers may happen to require. From the nature of his business, the retail dealer requires more capital and credit than the bill-broker pure and simple, because it may sometimes happen that his goods may remain on his counter for more or less time, until they happen to suit the fancy of a purchaser. His capital, however, is, as a rule, small

when compared with the volume of his turnover, and he depends on credit, most of which is advanced by the banks, for the financing of the bills of which he daily remains the holder. It will be remembered that the banks habitually have considerable sums lent to bill-brokers "at call and short notice," and that these loans were described as their second line of defence, as being most easily called in. Their first line of defence, as need hardly be repeated, is their holding of "cash in hand and at the Bank of England."

(3) Out of the retail dealer in bills has grown the discount house, an institution which still does a certain amount of retail business, but is at the same time in a position, owing to larger capital and more extended credit, to "run a much bigger book," as the jargon of the craft would phrase it; that is, the discount house is to a greater extent a permanent holder of bills and depends in a minor degree on the momentary fluctuations in the price of credit. Nevertheless, the discount houses are very large users of borrowed money, and regularly announce rates which they allow to depositors, these being generally slightly above the rates offered by the banks. Owing to this fact, of the slightly better rate allowed by them, they generally have the control of a considerable amount, placed on deposit with them by merchants and financiers, but at the same time, though their dependence on credit supplied

by the banks is not as great as in the case of the retail dealer in bills, it is still sufficient to make a serious difference to their operations, whenever the banks have occasion to reduce their loans.

Having thus, for the sake of being perspicuous, classified and distinguished the three kinds of dealers in bills, we may proceed to eliminate the real bill-broker, the almost obsolete dealer on commission, and to apply the term bill-broker to the two classes who have grown out of him and are still called by his name, in accordance with the consistently illogical manner in which the City applies titles and descriptions.

As we have seen, the distinction between the other two classes is solely one of degree, the degree being the extent to which they hold bills permanently, and depend for financing their operations on credit obtained from the banks. At the head of the body stand some few private firms of old standing, great wealth and first-rate credit, side by side with two big companies which have applied the joint-stock system with considerable success to the business of dealing in bills, and an old firm which has now been joint-stocked, but whose capital is held privately and in few hands. Under this leadership the market is compact and well-organized. The business is one which requires exceptional abilities and alertness, and the market rate of discount in London is perhaps the most sensitive and trustworthy barometer of international monetary conditions.

It was stated in the last chapter that the market rate is regulated in normal times by the banks, and we have now seen more clearly why this should be so, having found that the bill-brokers depend to a great extent on the banks both to supply them with credit and to buy bills from them. Nevertheless, though the average level of the rate is thus regulated, the action of the bill-brokers themselves has an important influence on its daily fluctuations and so may make a considerable difference to the movements of the foreign exchanges.

In order to realize the complicated nature of the problem that has to be solved by a bill-broker whenever he buys or sells a bill, let us endeavour to enumerate some of the chief considerations which determine his judgment on the points that have to be borne in mind. We will suppose he is offered a line of first-class paper due in three months' time, the present date being the last week in June.

But first it will be necessary to try to get a clear understanding of the meaning of the terms in which the discount market expresses the conduct of its business.

We will suppose then that the bill is offered to the broker at 4 per cent., that is to say, that 4 per cent. per annum is the rate of interest which is deducted from the face value of the bill, which it will realize in three months' time, in order to induce him to give cash for it. In other words, he is asked to give £99 to-day for each £100 in the amount that he will receive on presentation of the bill on maturity. As the calculation of discounts is very puzzling to the uninstructed inquirer, perhaps it is better to be still more arithmetically elementary, and point out that as three months is a quarter of a year, the 4 per cent. per annum is divided by four to arrive at the discount for three months, and hence it is that since the current discount rate is 4 per cent., we must knock £1 off each £100 of the bill's face value on maturity in order to arrive at its cash value on this basis. This rough calculation is only an illustration, of course, and the bill-broker, or his clerks, will work the problem out much more finely on the actual number of days in the bill. What has to be made clear is the fact that a bill is a security with a price, just like the stocks dealt in and quoted on the Stock Exchange, but that, instead of quoting the cash price for it, the market quotes the discount or the difference between its cash price and its face value on maturity. It is quite reasonable and simple when one thinks it out, that an instrument that will realize £100 in three months' time should only be worth £99 at the present moment, if 4 per cent. per annum be a fair rate to cover the probable fluctuations in the value of money in the meantime. But the number of people who have never taken the trouble to work out this elementary but tiresome problem, and consequently flounder when they think or talk about the discount market, is a continual astonishment, and must be my excuse for giving so much space to a statement which is about as informing as $1 + 1 = 2$.

Another frequent cause of confusion in this connection, though it also is dissolved by a moment's thought, arises out of the fact that the market is described as firm when discount rates go up, that is, when the price of the bill goes down. A firm discount market would result, we will suppose, in a rise in the discount rate from 4 to 4¼ per cent., and the result of this would be that the cash value of a bill with a year to run (for the sake of simplicity) would fall from 96 to 95¾. It is quite clear and reasonable that if money is more valuable the present price of a bill that will not mature for a year becomes less, because the buyer is giving immediate cash in return for the promise of cash a year hence. But to people who are accustomed to the expressions current on the Stock Exchange the notion of a firm market resulting in a fall in the price of the securities handled in it is often very confusing, for on the Stock Exchange, when they talk of a firm market, they mean one in which there is a strong demand for the securities handled by it and a consequent rise in prices. When the

Consols market is firm Consols go up, when the discount market is firm bills go down, which is only another way of saying that discount, which is the commodity in which the market really deals, goes up.

All this is very platitudinous, but I have known an occasion on which a financial journalist was taken to task, by a man of high standing in the City, for stating in his money article that the discount market was weak, with easier rates, owing to the scarcity of bills. In this case a practical banker of many years' experience had fallen into this trap, so that I must be excused for giving a considerable amount of space to the endeavour to warn less well-informed inquirers against it. A moment's thought shows that when bills are scarce and in demand, buyers who want them will have to take them at lower rates, that is, at higher prices, so that the newspaper statement objected to was perfectly correct.

Having done our best to put a fence round this tiresome pitfall, let us return to our bill-broker, who is still wondering whether to buy a parcel of three months' bills at 4 per cent. in the last week of June, and let us examine a few of the principal factors that will determine his decision.

In the first place he has to consider the immediate circumstances of the market and the prospect of his being able to resell the bills immediately at a profit, or to finance them comfortably if he be obliged to retain them.

The last week of June is a most unencouraging period from this point of view. The close of the two halves of the year are habitually marked by two processes, both of which severely restrict the supply of credit and of cash. In the last week of June and the last week of December an enormous volume of actual payments is made throughout the country, increasing materially the demands on all the banks for cash, and, at the same time, a large number of firms and companies, including some of the banks themselves, are making preparations for their half-yearly balance-sheets, that is to say, reducing credits granted to customers, and so increasing the proportion of their holdings of cash. As there is not enough cash to meet these two demands, it is nearly always necessary for the Bank of England to fill the gap; and in the period immediately preceding the turn of the two half-years it is usual for borrowers to go to the Bank of England and obtain credits with it for sums which sometimes amount to fifteen or twenty millions. Part of these credits is used for the withdrawal of actual currency, notes and gold, for the cash payments that have to be made all over the country; the rest is left to the credit of the borrower—or some one to whom he transfers it—in the books of the Bank of England, and the financial community is thus enabled to show a fine round sum of "cash in hand and at the Bank of England," a credit in the Bank of England's books being universally regarded as quite as good as, and much safer than, so many sovereigns in the pocket.

Our bill-broker, of course, has no need to think of all this; it is all so well known to him that it is part of his being. But it is a very important factor in the problem that he is debating. For the first consequence that arises is the probability, or certainty, that he will be unable to resell the bills to the banks, or to other regular buyers. At such a season, the banks are most unlikely to increase the number of their bills, and will probably not even replace those that fall due and are paid off. They will have a considerable stock of bills in their portfolios bought with a view to the cash demands at the end of the half-year and maturing within this very week; and the maturity of this paper will be one of their weapons in providing the cash that they will require for their customers and themselves.

Since, then, the bills under consideration by the bill-broker will not be easily convertible into immediate cash, he is faced by the problem of having to finance them himself. And from what has been said above it is clear that during the next few days this is likely to be an expensive matter.

As we have already seen, the bill-brokers depend largely on a supply of credit from the banks for financing their business, and our friend has, in all probability, been already apprised by his bankers and other providers of credit that they have, at the present moment, other uses for their funds. For the advances to bill-brokers have been described as the banks' second line of defence, and when they wish to increase their first line, which is their cash in hand and at the Bank of England, or to maintain it when it is diminished by their customers' demand for currency, they at once do so by calling in these loans to bill-brokers. So that far from expecting to be able to obtain the wherewithal, from ordinary sources, for financing the parcel that is offered, the bill-broker in question is probably already severely pinched in the matter of credit, and knows that if he takes these bills he will have to borrow from the Bank of England in order to pay for them. And borrowing from the Bank of England is an expensive operation, since it usually charges, for advances, ½ per cent. above its official discount rate, which, again, is almost always well above the loan rates current in the outside market.

So much for the adverse aspect of the immediate conditions. Against them we have to set the keenness of the seller, which induces him to offer an exceptionally fine parcel of bills at a rate which is tempting to the buyer, a high rate, that is to say, which means a low price for the bills ; also the fact that as most buyers of bills are cramped in the matter of credit by the seasonal demands already alluded to, and so are not in a position to compete eagerly for them, the present moment is a time in which the bold bargain-hunter, prepared to face the inconveniences of the moment, can often reap fine profits by the exercise of a capacity for disregarding immediate loss.

The forbidding appearance of the immediate conditions thus works both ways. In order to take the bills the broker knows that he will have to borrow from the Bank of England for at least a week, and that the higher rate paid for this temporary accommodation will make a hole in the profit that he hopes to make on the bill during the course of its currency; but if future prospects are inviting he will be willing enough to do this, and it is the future prospect that will sway his decision.

And now the vastness of the problem really begins to open itself out, and our broker, if of an imaginative turn of mind, may well fancy himself like a doubtful partisan, standing on a hill-top and vainly trying to peer through thick mists, with the aid of a somewhat inefficient spy-glass, into a great plain in which a battle is being waged by a number of forces of shifting and incalculable strength, and knowing that his life depends on throwing in his lot with the winning side.

In the immediate future there lies the probability

of a spell of cheap money, when the usual reaction takes place after the satisfaction of the temporary demands at the end of the half-year, and after the distribution of the dividends on Government stocks early in July, which results in transferring to the hands of the ordinary banks some four or five millions previously held by the Bank of England on behalf of the Government. These millions then become available at the market rate for loans, instead of at Bank rate, or ½ per cent. above it. After that, according to the normal tendency of the year's monetary history, the demands of holiday-makers and harvesters at home ought to begin to tell; while the great demand for currency all over the world, which generally shows itself during the autumn, when the crops of the chief agricultural countries are being gathered and garnered and shipped to the consumers' markets, ought just to be showing its force during the latter period of the currency of the bills offered, so that their date of maturity should be happy, enabling the holder to replace them on favourable terms.

According to the normal behaviour of monetary events, the buyer of a bill at a good price at the end of June ought thus to be able to reckon on a short spell of ease during which he would be able to finance his purchase on very favourable terms—perhaps getting his money at 2 per cent. against the bill which we suppose him to have bought at

4 per cent.—and a gradually hardening tendency, which should not, however, reduce him to the necessity of giving more for his money than he was earning on his bill, or being obliged to sell his bill at a loss, owing to inability to provide the wherewithal to carry it.

But it need not be said that monetary events do not habitually move along the lines of normal behaviour, and even along these lines a little swerve in one direction or another may suffice to upset calculations that have to be reduced to the fine terms required by the keen competition of the discount market in London. The slackening of general trade may greatly reduce the demands of commercial customers on the banks, and so throw a mass of credit back on them which they will pour out among the bill-brokers at nominal rates; a quickening of trade may have an equally marked effect in the other direction and upset all expectations of the spell of easy money which was to have made the holding of the bills a profitable transaction. A cold, wet summer will check holiday travel and expenditure, while a brilliant season will send a shower of currency through tourists' pockets into the hands of hotel-keepers and others who provide for their wants; and the extent of this outward tide will be among the innumerable items that will affect the volume of what is called money in Lombard Street. The quality and date of the harvest is another matter that affects the monetary position, and in calculating its probabilities the weather has once more to be allowed for; for if at the harvest season something like an ideal English summer is reigning, and farmers think that they can rely on the continuance of favourable skies, they will proceed leisurely and gradually, and the supply of currency that they will require be so much the less; but if the season is capricious, and a burst of harvesting weather arrives, everybody will want to save his crop at once, and each farmer will be pouring all the labour that he can get on to his fields and wanting money for wages, and for all the other expenditure that moving a crop entails.

And when he has balanced, as well as he can, the chances of trade, travel, and harvest requirements, the bill-broker must not forget the possible effects of an equally elusive factor, namely, the demands of Government finance; these do not, as a rule, count heavily at the period during which the parcel of bills offered is supposed to be current; as we shall see in a later chapter, it is in the January to March quarter, when the income-tax is being gathered, that the money market is habitually pinched by the transfer of cash to the Government's balance at the Bank of England; but throughout the year it is always possible that the Treasury will intervene with some unexpected demand in the shape of an issue of Treasury bills, or, on the other hand, may make money unexpectedly plentiful by allowing its balances to run below their normal level. For owing to the fact that the Bank of England is the Government's banker, the Government's money is in its hands, and consequently when the Government holds an unusually large sum, there is so much locked up, and not available in the outside market. So that the amount of the Government balances is always one of the items in the monetary problem, and the difficulty of calculating it is increased by the Olympian aloofness with which the Treasury conducts its operations—far away from the chaffering and huckstering of the market which it often affects so profoundly—and also by the Oriental mystery in which the movements of Government finance are shrouded.

And as if weather, trade, and Government finance were not sufficiently incalculable factors in the problem, there arises the purely psychological question of the possible extent of speculation on the Stock Exchange. We have seen that the banks, which supply the bill-broker with money, employ a considerable amount of the credit that they make and handle, in financing the requirements of those who buy stocks and shares and pay for them with borrowed money. Consequently, if an unusually large number of people come to the conclusion that a purchase of securities with borrowed money is likely to be profitable, the supply of money available for the bill-broker may be curtailed. And the reasons which suddenly impel the public to indulge in one of its periodical outbursts of speculation are, perhaps, as complicated a psychological problem as anybody could ever be asked to solve.

And yet we are still only on the threshold of the bill-broker's difficulty.

For all these things happen, or do not happen, at home and more or less under his own eye, and when he proceeds, as he must, to consider the possibility of foreign demands, he is face to face with questions which are much more difficult to answer and much more important in their effects. The movement of currency into the country for harvesting and holiday purposes, or the piling up of the Government's balance at the Bank, or the demands arising out of an unexpected outburst of speculation, may cause inconvenience, and perhaps, if their effects are particularly unanimous and untoward, make a serious difference to the profit on a bill: but a sudden foreign demand and a considerable export of gold might easily be followed by a complete alteration in the whole aspect of the market—a rise in Bank rate and a readjustment, for the time being, of the value of credit at home and abroad.

Having devoted so much space to the consideration of the bill-broker's problem, and having discovered that we have only touched the surface of it, it seems wiser on the whole to leave him with his problem and our sympathy. For any attempt to enter in detail into the innumerable causes which affect the demand for money abroad would lead us into a discourse of most formidable area.

But it may be mentioned incidentally that the risks of foreign politics and of international friction, the mere hint of which is often sufficient to affect the sentiment of the money market, are among the items in the enigma which has to be solved, or guessed at, by our bill-broker before he arrives at his decision. And it need not be said that any serious shock to credit occurring in any part of the commercially civilized world might easily upset all his calculations.

It is not, of course, implied that all these matters are actually revolved by a bill-broker before he makes up his mind about any of the numerous transactions which make up his day's business. If this were so, the work of the discount market would never get itself done. But they, and many more, are the data on which he has to work, and a rough-and-ready view of the balance of all these possibilities and hypotheses has to be at the back of his head somewhere in his sub-conscious intelligence.

The essential difference between him and the banker lies in the fact that the banker makes credit, while the broker sells credit, relying on being able to buy it cheaper. The conditions most favourable to the broker are a high discount rate, which is the price of the credit that he sells, and a low rate for money, or short loans, which are the credit that he buys. The broker has need of keen and sensitive alertness as opposed to the level-headed sagacity which is the most necessary asset of the banker. But the most important feature in the position of the bill-broker is that he constitutes the second line of the banker's defence, and consequently first feels the effect of any monetary pinch. If money is wanted suddenly by other customers whom bankers think fit to oblige, or if it is thought necessary to restrict the supply of money, the advances from bankers to bill-brokers are likely to be straightway curtailed. And this is an additional reason which makes a large supply of alert and open-eyed intelligence so necessary for his success.

CHAPTER IX

THE ACCEPTING HOUSES AND FOREIGN BANKS

It ought by this time to be clear, unless the proportion of the perspicuity of this work to its tediousness has been most lamentably inadequate, that what we call money generally means credits with a bank, and that most of these are created either out of loans made by the bank or by some other bank, or by the discounting of a bill, which is only a special form of loan.

Further, the bill has been shown to have advantages over any other form of security, because the shortness of its currency ensures a speedy return of his cash to the holder, and because it is drawn, or ought to be, against actual produce moving into consumption, so that, as is claimed by those who deal in it, a good bill of exchange pays itself.

It will also be remembered that the original bill of exchange was an order drawn on the purchaser of the produce by the seller, instructing him to pay its price to himself or some other party at the end of a period during which the purchaser might be expected to have disposed of the produce, either in its original form or worked up for consumption by some process of manufacture. And the purchaser of the goods accepted the bill by signing his name across it—that is, acknowledged that he would be liable for the sum named at the due date, and so became the acceptor of the bill. After which the bill, drawn by a good name and accepted by a good name, and with the necessary documents in order showing that goods had been duly shipped and insured, was as sound and attractive a security as the most sceptical money-lender could require, and could readily be discounted and advanced against.

It is necessary to pick up these threads which we left flying loose when we turned from the consideration of the forms of money to that of the principal wheels in the machine which produces money. Of these we have found that the banks are the chief, since they provide the right to draw cheques, which are the currency of English commerce, and give credits against indebtedness, which is called into being by the fact that trade habitually lives on the profits which it is in process of realizing, and could not proceed with its present unceasing velocity if it had to wait for their realization before it went on to its next task. Next we examined the operations and responsibilities of the bill brokers, the retail dealers in bills, who are, as it were, an offshoot of the banks specializing on the selection of bills to suit the requirements of the bankers as to date, etc., and keeping them in stock with the assistance of credits chiefly furnished by the banks. It is now necessary to consider the functions of those who manufacture the bills, against which the banks and discount houses jointly or severally provide credits.

In describing the bill of exchange in Chapter IV. we took the simplest possible case in order to keep the ground as clear as might be of confusing obstructions, and imagined an American farmer, Mr. Silas P. Watt, selling wheat to a London merchant, Mr. John Smith, and drawing a bill on him for the value of the produce. By so doing we not only attained a measure of clearness which would otherwise have been impossible, but also got down to the ultimate facts of the case. For the real manufacturers of real produce bills are still the grower of the produce and the merchant who handles it in its ultimate market. Without them the produce could not come into existence, and without produce there could be no bills, except of the kite-flying order, as drawn by Mr. Micawber on Mrs. Micawber.

Nevertheless, modern processes of specialization have introduced certain intermediaries between the producer and the merchant in the ultimate market. As matters are arranged now Mr. Watt would sell his wheat to a merchant in his own country, and it would probably pass through many hands on paper before it was finally shipped. It would be financed in the mean time by advances from American banks, and the bill drawn against it, when finally shipped, would be drawn by an American bank or finance house on its correspondents in London, who would be a firm devoting much if not most of its time and attention to this specialized industry of acceptance.

Since this inquiry is confined to the machinery of money in London, we can leave out the producer and the American merchant and their bankers and confine ourselves to the London end of the bill, that is, the London name which is written across it, and so marks it as accepted.

It is easy to understand how a distinct class of accepting houses grew up out of the merchant importers who originally accepted bills in the course of their importing business, that is, accepted orders on themselves to pay for goods which were in process of being forwarded to them. The readiness with which the acceptances of the different merchants would be discounted and turned into cash would vary considerably with the difference in their reputation and standing, and the caution with which they were credited in the matter of conducting their business. And the varying readiness with which certain acceptances were discounted would inevitably express itself in varying rates at which their bills could be placed. It would thus naturally follow that it would profit merchants of second-rate standing to give a commission to those whose reputation was more exalted in order to secure a more attractive signature than their own, and so get back the commission and a little more by being able to finance their operations more cheaply than by means of their own acceptance.

The merchants of first-class credit would thus find that they could let out the use of their reputations on profitable terms, and proceed to specialize in this branch of business, which consisted in examining into the bills put before them for acceptance, keeping themselves well acquainted with the means and standing of the drawers of them, and giving their acceptance, for a commission, to such paper as fulfilled the requirements of their discrimination.

The foreign connections arising out of the original trading operations, with which they laid the first foundations of their mercantile position, naturally led these houses into providing monetary accommodation for the governments of the countries with which they traded, and there thus grew up out of the ranks of successful City merchants a class of merchant bankers, financiers and accepting houses, which, along with the old private banking houses, constituted a sort of aristocracy in the City, which still survives to some extent. They are often described as merchant bankers, but it is important to remember that they are not bankers in the strict sense of the term—that is, they do not pay cash across the counter against cheques drawn on them—because it is from their ranks that the directors of the Bank of England are chiefly recruited, and as we shall see in a later chapter, a director of the Bank of England must not be a banker.

The importance of the function of the accepting house need not be emphasized. If the producer of the produce is the original creator of the bill, it is the acceptor who, by his signature, gives it currency and hall-marks it for the purposes of the London market. A banker or broker who discounts a bill and parts with cash or credit in exchange for it, cannot be expected always to know the position and trustworthiness of the drawer, and must often rely on the name of the acceptor as his sole guide in appraising its merit. So that it is by the judicious and properly regulated use of their names that the accepting houses put into circulation an enormous mass of credit instruments, the supreme merits of which as liquid investments have already been insisted on with "damnable iteration."

Nevertheless, the office of the accepting houses is still dependent on that of the banks, because the bills that they accept, though thereby greatly furthered in their progress towards becoming cash, do not actually become cash until they have been discounted. And this is done either by a banker or by a bill-broker, who works with credit, generally furnished to him by a banker. A bill that cannot be discounted is of no use to the holder until its day of maturity, and is not until then a credit instrument in any sense. And we thus come back once more to the supreme importance of the banks in London's monetary polity.

For the power of the accepting houses to give currency, by their acceptance, to paper concerning the merits of which they are best in a position to discriminate, is one that is obviously liable to dangerous abuse, and in their case the check of publicity is absent, since the private nature of their business keeps it free even from the ceremony of a half-yearly published balance-sheet. A very little carelessness, and very little error on the side of optimism, and a very little neglect of the principle that the basis of a real bill should be real produce moving into consumption, and there are all the materials for a dangerous inflation of credit. And the banks, which ultimately provide the means by which acceptances are turned into cash or credit, have thus an important responsibility thrown upon them, and one which is not apparent to the general public, to which the whole machinery of acceptance is more or less a mystery.

The question is complicated by the fact that, as has already been mentioned, the banks have themselves undertaken the business of acceptance to an extent that has increased rapidly in recent years.

The excellent sanity with which the banks conduct their business makes this complication more apparent than real; and the dependence of the accepting houses on the good opinion of the cheque-paying banks concerning their paper is modified by the fact that they can ultimately have recourse to the Bank of England, through a bill broker. The Bank of England requires two London names on bills that it discounts, and a bill accepted by a London firm and endorsed by a London bill-broker fulfils its requirements. And the Bank of England has before now intervened with effect when the paper of an accepting house has been unreasonably considered too plentiful by the other banks.

Nevertheless, the opinion of the banks concerning the paper of an accepting house is very important to it; and the position is curious which makes the banks at once the watch-dogs over the volume of acceptance, and large, increasingly large, acceptors themselves. It is possible that, in the early days of their experience in this line of business, the banks gave their acceptance too cheaply, and it is natural that the accepting houses should regard their intrusion into it with an unfavourable eye. It is also very essential that the banks should remember that the least irregularity or carelessness on their part in the selection of the paper that they hall-mark with their acceptance might have very far-reaching effects, if it came to light and were the subject of City comment, because the general body of their customers and depositors would be extremely likely to misunderstand it; and that what would be a mere indiscretion in an accepting house, which does not depend for its existence on the confidence of the uninstructed multitude, might mean disaster to a bank, which does.

At the same time, if watched over with due care, the growing interest of the banks in acceptance business seems to be a perfectly natural process arising out of the increasing requirements of the expanding trade of the world. It is difficult for the ranks of the old accepting houses to be recruited; it has lately been done with success, but a firm that enters on the business has to have capital and credit at its command, such as are rarely to be found in the hands of folk who are prepared to risk them in a new enterprise, the technicalities of which have to be acquired with patience, and perhaps through costly experience. The extent to which the old houses can accept is restricted by the obvious limits which are imposed on the amount of business, especially of business in credit, that can be done by any one firm. And the reputation and position of the banks seem to qualify them naturally to fill the gap.

An important part of the machinery of acceptance is also furnished by the Indian and Colonial banks, which, naturally again, give a large part of their attention to providing exchange between London and the country with which they are connected, and to handling the paper which its trade calls into being. The high reputation of the Indian banks, and the skill with which the bills endorsed by them are marketed, makes the prices fetched by their bills often a leading factor in the quotations of the discount market.

Finally, in considering the main springs which feed the flood of acceptance, we come to the London agencies of the chief Continental banks, which play a very important part both as sellers and buyers of bills. Foreign financiers were quick to detect the advantages of the English credit system, and to turn them to their own profit and to the furtherance of the trade of the countries that they represent. It is often contended that the rapid expansion of German trade, which pushed itself largely by its elasticity and adaptability to the wishes of its customers, could never have been achieved if it had not been assisted by cheap credit furnished in London, by means of which German merchants ousted English manufactures with offers of long credit facilities to their foreign customers.

An instructive example of this system of pushing business on credit, and of its disastrous results to all parties when carried too far, was lately furnished by the embarrassments of German traders with Japan. A letter from the Tokio correspondent of the *Economist*, dated May 8, and published on May 30, 1908, dealt with the financial and commercial strain and depression then ruling in Japan, and its adverse effect on foreign (non-Japanese) merchants, and proceeded, in the following passage:—

"Almost all the foreign firms thus far affected are German, and the reason is not far to seek. Years ago, the Japanese import trade was chiefly carried on upon a cash basis. A Japanese merchant gave an order for goods, against which he deposited bargain money, and when the merchandise arrived he took delivery only after paying the balance. The German merchants, however, gradually introduced a credit system. First the goods were permitted to be taken away, and payment deferred until they reached the go-downs of the Japanese purchaser, this concession being made on the quite reasonable plea that, as soon as the latter had the goods in his possession, he would be able to get advances on them from the native banks, and liquidate his account. But the time limit was gradually extended . . . until delivery was permitted to be taken against promissory notes for as long as from three to six months. Though the British merchants stood out against the practice as long as possible, they were compelled to follow suit to some extent; but, holding that such an extension of credit was dangerous in Japan, they never went so far as their German competitors. So long as things went well in this country the credit system worked satisfactorily, and during the boom after the war, there can be no doubt that the business handled by the Germans went ahead more rapidly than that in the hands of British merchants, who preferred to work on the old conservative lines. As soon, however, as a period of stringency in money and contraction in trade took place, difficulties began to arise . . . Very heavy losses have been suffered. It is not too much to say that in the last six months the German merchants have lost far more than they gained during the two years of the boom by the extension of the credit system. Once more it has been shown that unsound methods of doing business, whatever advantage they may bring for the moment, are disastrous in the long run."

This instructive message is an example of much that has been happening in many other countries besides Japan, Morocco having been another field in which seed of this sort is believed to have been plentifully sown. No one can quarrel with the Germans for making use of the credit weapon in extending their trade, though their over-extension of credit facilities has had results which fall on others besides themselves; still less can they be blamed for their cleverness in taking full advantage of London's monetary machinery, and providing themselves in London with the credit with which they wheedled away England's customers in countries where credit facilities were an attractive novelty, over-indulgence in which has since proved unwholesome both for the giver and the taker.

It is very probable that the extent to which they did so is much exaggerated, since in a case of this kind, in which figures are necessarily not available, an active imagination roams at large. But it is at least interesting to note that England, having done so much to establish the foundations of German military and political greatness at the time of Frederick the Great, when it subsidized the young kingdom of Prussia at a critical period in its Titanic struggle,* has also given a helping hand to German trade with the facilities so cheaply offered by the London discount market.

Let us hope that our German friends are duly grateful, and let us avoid the mistake of imagining that we have done ourselves any permanent harm by this assistance. It is to the economic interest of humanity at large that production should be stimulated, and the economic interest of humanity at large is the interest of England with its mighty world-wide trade. Germany has quickened production with the help of English credit, and so, it may be remarked, has every economically civilized country in the world. The fact that all or most of them, including our own colonies, develop their resources with the help of English capital and credit, and then do their utmost to keep out our products by means of tariffs, makes it appear to superficial observers that England provides capital for the destruction of its own business. But, in practice, the system works quite otherwise. For all these countries that develop their resources with our money, aim at developing an export trade and

* Carlyle, "Frederick the Great," book xviii. chapter 11.

selling goods to us, and as they have not yet reached the point of economic altruism at which they are prepared to sell goods for nothing, the increase in their production means an increasing demand for our commodities and services. And in the mean time the interest on our capital and credit, and the profits on working the machinery of exchange, are a comfortable addition to our national income.

This digression is not quite as irrelevant as it seems, for there is a strong feeling among the manufacturing classes that the facilities given by the London money market to foreign borrowers are detrimental to English trade. This contention cannot be set aside as lightly as it sometimes is by the defenders of our banking system. The obvious answer to it is that England makes profits out of its credit factory which very much more than compensate it for any handicap imposed on its manufactures of other commodities. But it must be admitted that this is only a partial answer, and that if the handicap were real and persistent, its working would tend to make England a banking, discounting and exchange-dealing nation rather than a manufacturing nation; in other words, it would tend to turn our energies into financing, calculating, and book-keeping, rather than producing and working on commodities. This process would not necessarily be an evil, but is a matter which might have important economic and social results, and ought not to be ignored if it were really at work. The organization of foreign banking which places credit facilities, borrowed in London, at the disposal of foreign manufacturers, is a matter which calls for respectful imitation in England. There ought to be no possible ground for the assertion, which is sometimes heard, that English traders cannot borrow in their own market as cheaply as foreigners. A remedy for this evil, if it really exists, would be merely a matter of organization and co-operation between our mercantile and banking communities, and its further discussion is obviously out of place in a merely explanatory work.

This excursion into complicated questions of international trade was necessitated by the appearance of the agencies of foreign banks as an important item among the institutions whose acceptances give currency to bills of exchange and enable them to be discounted or sold for cash. They also at times have an important influence on discount rates by dealing on the other side of the market and buying English bills. And both these operations, whether they raise credits on this side by selling their own bills, or obtain a credit due at a later date by buying and holding English bills, give them a hold on London's gold. In fact, their holding of English bills is arranged with this direct object. Some Continental institutions always keep a portfolio stocked with bills on London, constantly replaced as they mature, so that in time of need they may take gold from London to replenish the basis of their note issues. And this fact is one that obviously has to be continually remembered and allowed for by the directors of the Bank of England, which has London's store of gold in its keeping. And moreover, the dealings of foreign houses in bills of exchange have an important effect on the foreign exchanges, and bring us face to face with the necessity for an explanation of that formidable subject.

CHAPTER X

THE FOREIGN EXCHANGES

THE foreign exchanges are really a fairly simple matter if we keep them free, as far as possible, from the technicalities which are the delight of experts in the subject, who generally expound it. They were exemplified in Chapter I. by the purchase of a postal order, and they may be described as the mechanism by which money here is exchanged for money somewhere else. In the example there given the business was simplified by the existence of the machinery of the Post Office, which is prepared to undertake exchange transactions at fixed rates.

In the exchanges of the large amounts which international commerce makes payable in one place or another, the bill of exchange plays an important part. But the essential point to be grasped is the fact that fluctuations in rates of exchange are caused by variations in the relative value in the currencies of the two centres between which the exchange is quoted. If a large number of Londoners have payments to make in Paris, or want to send money to Paris, a large number of people will want to exchange sovereigns for francs, and the value of the sovereign will be depreciated when expressed in francs, and the Paris exchange will move "against London." The most obvious reasons which will cause this variation, or stimulate this demand in London for remittances to Paris, will be the balance of trade in its widest sense—the exchange of commodities and all kinds of services between England and France—and the rate of interest ruling in the two centres. If Paris sells more goods and services to London, more people in London will have payments to make in Paris; and if the rate of interest be 3 per cent. in Paris and 2 per cent. in London, money will tend to flow from London to Paris to earn the higher rate, and the demand for remittances to Paris will thus be further stimulated.

Since bills of exchange play an important part in this business of the exchanges, it is perhaps safer to repeat here that a bill of exchange is an order by A directing B to pay a sum of money to himself, A, or to a third party; that the cheque with which you tell your bank to pay £2 to your butcher is, in fact, a bill of exchange; but that the term, in its more usual meaning, implies an order on a person at some distance in space to pay a sum at some distance in time. As, for example, when a dairy farmer in New South Wales sells butter to a produce merchant in London, and draws a bill on him at sixty days' sight. When the bill is "accepted"—

that is, when the merchant acknowledges his liability to pay by writing his signature across the bill—it becomes a negotiable instrument and can be discounted and turned into cash.

It can also, evidently, be used wherewith to pay any debts that the farmer may have to meet in London. If he owes a similar sum to his harness dealer, he can hand the bill over to him and let him collect the money from the merchant; and the one bill will thus have paid two debts. It has paid the farmer on behalf of the produce merchant, and the harness dealer on behalf of the farmer. Or if the farmer owes money in other parts of the world, a bill on London is always acceptable; if he has bought hay-making machinery in America, the draft on his merchant could be used equally well to pay for it, for there would be plenty of people in the United States who have payments to make in London and will give a certain number of American dollars to the manufacturer of mechanical hay-makers for his order on the London merchant.

And here comes in the difficulty which makes the foreign exchanges apparently so obscure. When it was a matter of a payment between London and Sydney, there was no question of a difference of currency, for in both these places the sovereign is the unit in which payments are expressed. But when a draft on London has to be sold in America, the relative value of the sovereign and the dollar comes into the calculation. And the unfamiliar observer is puzzled by the fact that these relative values continually fluctuate, with the result that the table of exchange quotations constantly varies, and the exchanges are said to move in favour of or against a particular country in a manner which is very extraordinary to him, since the intrinsic value of the currencies that they represent is unaltered.

We shall arrive at a clearer understanding of the matter if we leave out for the present this question of exchange of different currencies and return to that of the exchange between London and Sydney. These two towns use the same coin of the same fineness as legal tender and as money of account, and therefore it might be supposed that any one who has to make a payment of £20 in Sydney would have to put down in London exactly £20 plus a payment to the colonial banker who sells him the draft for his trouble and expense in sending the money.

But this is not so. Owing to the fact that Australia constantly has to remit to England in order to meet interest on debt, etc., the Australian exchange is normally in favour of England; that is to say, a credit on London is more sought after in Sydney than a credit on Sydney is sought after in London, because the drain of money is habitually from Sydney to London.

Hence, if you go to an Australian bank's London office and buy a draft on Sydney with your cheque on the Westminster Bank, you are giving it money in London in exchange for money in Sydney, and we have seen that money in London is relatively more valuable than money in Sydney owing to the exchange being normally in favour of London.

Consequently, the Australian bank is prepared not indeed to give you an order for £20 and something over in Sydney in return for your London cheque for £20, but to do what comes to the same thing, namely, manage your remittance for you for nothing, making no charge for its trouble.

But if the movement were reversed, and some one in Sydney were buying on London, he would have to pay £20 plus a premium, because the exchange is in favour of London; that is, a sovereign in London normally commands more than a sovereign when compared with a sovereign in Sydney.

Here, then, we have an example of the working of the laws of exchange between two countries in which the coins into which drafts are convertible are identical, and if once we can grasp the logic of this, we have gone a long way towards simplifying the more complicated question of the exchanges between countries with different currencies.

For the broad principle is the same everywhere. Whenever, for any reason, one place, A, has to send more money to another place, B, than B has to send to it, B's currency will be relatively more valuable, and the exchange will be in favour of B.

Let us consider the matter again in the case of Sydney and London and suppose that instead of going to one bank to arrange your remittance you went into a regular market wherein were assembled representatives of many Australian banks and exchange dealers, and waving your cheque on the Westminster before them asked them how much money in Sydney they would give for it. If the pressure to remit money from Sydney to London were keen, they would all be eager to have your London cheque, because by buying it in exchange for a draft on their Sydney balance they would be increasing their London credit at the expense of their Sydney credit without incurring the cost and risk of sending coin or bullion from Australia.

Consequently competition would impel them to give you something more than £20 in Sydney, but that something more would be limited by the expense of sending coin and bullion. If we suppose, for the sake of simplicity, that expense to be covered by *6d.* per pound, it would pay them if the demand were eager enough to give £20 10*s.* for your London cheque. Beyond that it would not pay them to go. If you tried to insist on £20 10*s.* 1*d.*, it would be cheaper for them to send coin from Australia. So that in this case £20 10*s.* (or

£1 0s. 6d. per pound) would represent what is called gold point, and if your London cheque really fetched that price, the exchange between London and Sydney would be said to have gone in favour of London up to gold point, and the movement of gold from Sydney to London might be expected to begin.

In the case of large amounts, and of places far distant, the element of time becomes important. If exchange between London and Sydney were at par, it might still pay an Australian banker to give more than a sovereign in Sydney for a sovereign in London because he would receive the sovereign in London at once, and his balance in Sydney would only be drawn on five weeks hence when the draft arrived. So that he would have the use of your money for five weeks, and in times when the rate of interest is high this is an important consideration.

In the example just considered, where the exchange between London and Sydney was strongly in favour of London, it was supposed that a sovereign, or a sovereign's worth of credit, in London might fetch £1 0s. 6d. in Sydney. If the tendency of the balance of indebtedness were flowing in the other direction, and there were a great demand for drafts payable in Sydney, London's currency would be depreciated as compared with Sydney's, and a sovereign here might only fetch 19s. 6d. on the other side. But this depreciation could only work up to the point at which it would pay those who have debts to pay in Sydney to pack sovereigns and send them rather than make use of the machinery of exchange. If you were offered only 19*s.* in Sydney in exchange for your sovereign here you would obviously inform the dealers in exchange that you preferred to dispense with their services, and would ship the sovereigns to your Australian creditor.

Restating the matter yet again in the effort to be clear, we may express it by saying when the number of people who want to send money from Sydney to London is greater than the number of those who want to send money from London to Sydney, the latter will be in an advantageous position, and able to buy drafts on favourable terms: but that the amount in Sydney that their sovereigns or cheques representing sovereigns in London will fetch cannot rise above the exact equivalent plus the cost of remitting coin from one centre to the other. When that point is reached the exchange is at gold point.

What is called the mint par between the two places is in this case the sovereign, and if the cost of remittance, insurance, etc., be 6*d.*, as we have supposed for the sake of simplicity, the outside fluctuation of the exchange will be 1*s.*; for if it cost Sydney over 20*s.* 6*d.* to buy a sovereign in

London, Sydney will ship gold to London rather than buy drafts; and if a sovereign in London fetch less than 19*s.* 6*d.* in Sydney, Sydney will import gold from London.

We can now proceed to consider the question as it appears when the balance of indebtedness is being settled between two countries which use a different currency.

In France the unit is the franc, so that when a Frenchman wants to send money to London he wants to exchange francs into sovereigns; conversely, an Englishman who wants to send money to Paris has to exchange sovereigns for francs.

The relative value of the two currencies measured in the amount of gold contained in the sovereign and the 20-franc piece is 25*f.* 22*c.* to the sovereign. The normal exchange or mint par is thus ruling when the Paris cheque is quoted at 25*f.* 22*c.*

The cost of sending gold in either direction may be taken at 7*c.*; so that if you ship gold each sovereign's worth of it will be worth to you in Paris 25*f.* 15*c.*, having shed 7*c.* on the way in expenses. Consequently, if you can buy a bill on Paris at any higher rate it will pay you to do so rather than send gold.

Whether you will be able to do so will depend on the value of money in Paris as compared with London, and on the balance of indebtedness between London and Paris. If the rate of interest is higher in Paris than in London, London will want to send money to Paris to earn the higher rate, and if Paris has been selling us more goods and securities and services than we have been selling to her, Paris will have more bills on London arising out of those sales than London has bills on Paris; consequently, the demand in London for bills on Paris will be keener than the demand in Paris for bills on London, because London has more remittances to make.

Hence it will follow that the seller of a bill on Paris will be able to get more favourable terms, and the exchange will be, as it is called, in his favour; in other words, his francs will be relatively more valuable than the sovereign, and the sovereign will fetch less when expressed in francs. And if the balance of indebtedness be heavy enough, and the competition of those who want to buy drafts on Paris—that is, to exchange sovereigns for francs—be keen enough, the value of sovereigns expressed in francs will go down to 25*f.* 15*c.*, and then those who have remittances to make will begin to ship gold instead of buying drafts, the Paris exchange having gone down to gold point.

When the balance is the other way, and London has been selling more goods and securities and services to Paris than Paris has been selling to London, bills on Paris will be more plentiful than bills on London, and the French importers of goods, etc., will have to compete for drafts on London in which to make their payments. That is, they will have to pay more in francs, which will be relatively depreciated, for the sovereigns that they need for the payment of their debts, and their competition will force the exchange up towards *25f. 29c.*, which will be the other gold point, when shipments of the metal may be expected. But it must not be forgotten that the relative value of money in the two centres is a constant influence which may increase or modify the movement of exchange due to the influence of indebtedness for goods and services. If London has sold large amounts of goods to Paris, but money is dear in Paris, the two influences will tend to counteract one another; London will leave the proceeds of its sales in Paris to earn the higher rate of interest, and as long as it does so those sales will not affect the exchange.

It may have been noted that the French exchange is against London when it is low and in London's favour when it is high. And this is natural and inevitable when we consider that the quotation expresses the value in francs which a sovereign will fetch. When this value is low the holder of a sovereign receives less in francs, and so the exchange is very literally against him. When you want to buy francs with your sovereign, the more francs you get for it the better it is for you. When the rates of exchange are quoted in English money, it is otherwise. The Argentine dollar is quoted in pence. When it rises from $48\frac{1}{4}$*d.* to $48\frac{3}{8}$*d.* it moves against England, because it fetches more pence, and any one who wants to exchange sovereigns for dollars will receive less of them. This is one of the small complications which make the question of the exchanges so difficult to the inexperienced. But it can always be met by considering that the ultimate fact expressed by rates of exchange is the relative value between a sovereign and a foreign currency. When the sovereign buys more of the foreign currency the exchange has moved in our favour; when it buys less the exchange has moved against us.

It thus becomes evident that the foreign exchanges are a mechanism by which international indebtedness is settled between one country and another, and that rates of exchange are the prices at which the currencies of the various countries are expressed relatively to one another. When the balance of claims between two places does not roughly agree gold has to be shipped to settle the difference, unless it can be met by what is called arbitrage, which consists of dealings in bills on other centres. For instance, London may not have enough claims on Paris to set off the claims of Paris on it, but may be able to fill the gap with bills on Berlin, or some other centre, which Paris may happen to want.

The system on which the exchanges work is thus similar to that of the bankers' Clearing house in London. In it the claims of the clearing banks are crossed off against one another, and any balance that is due, for example, from the Westminster Bank to the County, is settled by the deduction of part of the Westminster's credit at the Bank of England and its addition to the County's. But in the case of international indebtedness, the balances have to be settled by shipments of gold. Such, at least, is the theory of the matter, though the restrictions that most of the chief Continental centres place on withdrawals of gold often prevent, or at least postpone, the working of the machinery of exchange in accordance with theory.

The broad principle which has been thus set forth and exemplified is the ultimate basis of the movements in the rates of exchange between all countries, even those which have currencies based on different metals, or in the case of those in which the currency is based on nothing but the printing-press. But it need hardly be said that there can be no gold point in the case of countries with a currency which consists of silver or of inconvertible paper notes. Nevertheless, even in their case, though the fluctuation of exchange is complicated by variations in the price of silver or by new issues of paper currency, yet the balance of relative indebtedness between them and other countries is still an important factor, ready to assert its complete predominance at any moment when other complicating influences cease from troubling.

Since, then, it is largely on the mutual indebtedness of various countries that rates of exchange are based—though we must not forget the influence of the rate of interest in the various centres—let us see how this mutual indebtedness arises.

The most obvious cause of it is the mutual exchange of natural produce and manufactured articles—the balance of trade, as it is generally called. This we see chronicled in the monthly returns issued by the Board of Trade of British imports and exports. These always show that England has imported goods of much greater value than those which she has exported, and because there is no published record of her other exports—her invisible exports, as they are sometimes called—superficial observers are often very much frightened about the state of English trade and draw astonishing inferences, the most notable of which was propounded by a colonial premier who told an English audience that England had to export annually so many millions of golden sovereigns to pay for the balance of the cost of her imports over that of her exports.

In fact, an "unfavourable" balance of trade, which is the misleading description given to this condition of the purely commercial relations between one country and another, is one that can only be afforded by countries of the highest economic development which are in a position to supply other countries with credit and other services, which the other countries have to pay for with their goods. And the distinction of possessing an unfavourable trade balance is shared with England by France and Germany.

At the same time, those who are alarmed by the extent of the difference between the value of our visible exports and imports are justified to this extent, if they consider that it is better for England to be a manufacturing country than a creditor and banking country. A large part of our invisible exports consists of services rendered by the clerking and financing classes, and those critics of our trade position who do not ignore them, but maintain that they would prefer to see them replaced by goods worked up by the producing and manufacturing classes, take up an attitude which is perfectly logical. The more common course, however, is to ignore these invisible exports altogether, as was done by Mr. Seddon in the speech referred to above, and to deduce the alarming conclusion that we are living on our capital, and otherwise in a terribly decadent and deplorable condition, from the commercial point of view.

This being so, though it is an oft-told tale, it is perhaps worth while to enumerate some of the invisible exports by means of which we fill the big gap between the values of our imports and exports of visible goods.

Let us consider the case as it stands between us and the United States. The United States supply us with a vast and valuable amount of food and raw material, and take from us manufactured goods, the amount of which is severely restricted by their high Protectionist tariff. On the other hand, we export to them the following "invisible" items:—

(1) Shipping freights. Our ships carry goods to and from them all over the world.

(2) Interest coupons. The American securities held by English investors yield a constant income in interest, to meet which the United States has to send goods.

(3) Insurance facilities. The English insurance companies and firms do a large business in the United States, and draw thence a regular income in premiums.

(4) Banking facilities. The large sums spent annually by Americans in Continental travel are, to a great extent, financed by drafts on London, on which London takes toll. Still greater, probably, is the profit that London regularly makes by discounting bills for America, financing its speculations by carrying over shares for it in the London market, and making advances in other forms.

(5) Pleasure, social amenities, titles, and art treasures. Americans in times of prosperity spend a constantly increasing amount in travel and enjoyment in England. Many of them, it is said, are anxious to cut a figure in what is called Society, and the lavish expenditure in which they indulge is believed to be of some assistance to this ambition. All this expenditure here on their part has the same effect on the balance of Anglo-American indebtedness as an English export. It is also well known that the scions of ancient English families frequently find wives among the attractive daughters of America, and the big dowries that the latter bring with them amount to a considerable annual charge on the United States. The habit of purchasing art treasures, lately rife among rich Americans, is another item in the balance. The fact that owing to American tariff regulations many of these art treasures are left here does not, of course, interfere with the effect on international indebtedness produced by their purchase.

(6) Family affection. Many of the English, and especially Irish, settlers in America regularly remit sums to their parents and families in England, taking nothing in return but affection and gratitude. Every one who has read "Some Experiences of an Irish R.M." remembers the picture of McCarthy, the horse-dealing farmer who charged Mr. Bernard Shute £45 for a mare,

saying, "She's too grand entirely for a poor farmer like me, and if it wasn't for the long weak family I have, I wouldn't part with her for twice the money." The long weak family was explained by Mr. Flurry Knox to be "three fine lumps of daughters in America paying his rent for him."

The above list might be continued, but sufficient examples have been given to show that there are many more exports in heaven and earth than are dreamt of by the philosophy of the Board of Trade returns. It must not be supposed that the movement of these items is all in one direction. American ships carry English goods, American insurance offices do business in England, and Englishmen spend money on travel and sport in America. It is only claimed that on the above counts America normally owes more to England than England owes to America, and that credits under these heads go far to neutralize the so-called "unfavourable" balance of trade.

It need not, of course, be supposed that the final balance, after allowing for all exports and imports, visible and invisible, must be exactly equal between any two countries. It is perfectly possible for one country to be normally indebted to another year in, year out, on this balance of trade in its widest sense, and yet to be in a perfectly wholesome economic condition, being kept so by being in a contrary relation with some other country. It will thus be able to meet the bills drawn on it by its creditor with those that it draws on its debtor, and thus the sum of mutual indebtedness is crossed off and cancelled all over the world, or met, when at any time the supply of bills is inadequate, by movements of bullion to settle the balances.

This case arises, for example, when the chief agricultural countries are reaping and moving their crops. They hold, for the time being, the manufacturing countries in fee, and they need gold for the actual circulation of currency in the producing districts. And, consequently, gold moves normally to the United States, Egypt, and Argentina in their harvesting seasons.

It is in these cases that the utility arises of the practice, referred to in earlier chapters, of drawing bills in anticipation of crop movements. Without this arrangement, countries whose staple export is harvested at a certain season would take payment in gold for it at that season, and would, during the rest of the year, have to remit in gold for the goods and services that it buys from other countries. But the dealers in exchange, and the more legitimate class of finance bill,* provide the means by which, at times when such a country has nothing to export, the exchange dealers will make good profits by creating bills against nothing, but in anticipation of the crop that is in the ground, with the result that the country

* Page 48.

exports less gold in its off seasons, and imports less when its crop is ready. Its imports of machinery in July are paid for by semi-fictitious remittances, created by exchange dealers who draw finance bills and so raise credits, and these bills are met later by the shipment of the country's crops in September, and by the bills genuinely drawn against them. And so the clumsy necessity for sending gold backwards and forwards across the oceans is reduced, though not extinguished.

It need not be said that it is quite impossible to gauge the amount and value of the invisible commodities, which, as above enumerated, have so important an effect on the balance of international indebtedness, and so on the foreign exchanges. And one of the most elusive of the influences which thus complicate the question is that of the purchase and sale of securities between one country and another. But it has to be considered now because it is closely connected with the main question dealt with in this inquiry.

When one country raises a public loan in another, everybody is well aware of the transaction, and there is no difficulty about the matter. For example, Brazil borrows three millions in the London market by an issue of 5 per cent. bonds. The issue is advertised and subscribed, there is an open market in the bonds, and it is all clear and above-board. Brazil has exported to England three millions' worth of its promises to pay; England has returned to Brazil three millions' worth of money or credit, or the right to draw on London, either by taking gold or by using its credits here to cancel debt elsewhere, or to make any purchases required. The immediate effect of the transaction will be to turn the exchange in favour of Brazil, though it must always be remembered that the overt working of this effect may be veiled by other influences. During the currency of the loan the effect of its existence will be to turn the exchange in favour of London, because Brazil will be obliged to remit periodically to meet the quarterly or half-yearly interest payments or the service of the sinking fund established to extinguish the loan gradually by purchase or drawings of the bonds.

Hence it is that no debtor country—that is, no country which has borrowed extensively from the investors and money-lenders of other countries—can afford the luxury of what is called an unfavourable trade balance. In order to meet its interest payments and its sinking fund arrangements, it must habitually ship more goods than it receives, since the lenders are continually sending it interest coupons and drawn bonds, the payment of which it has to provide for either with goods or with fresh borrowing.

In other words, what is usually called a favourable trade balance may generally be taken as a sign of the economic dependence of the country which possesses it.

The same effect on the exchanges is produced when the borrowing is done, not by the Government of the borrowing country, but by companies; as, for example, when the Pennsylvania Railroad sells £4,000,000 bonds here, the operation for the moment turns the exchange in favour of the United States, but during the currency of the bonds produces a periodical claim by London on New York for interest payments.

These public issues of loans are potent and obvious influences on the exchange. But an equally important effect, which is difficult to trace, is produced by the purchases of securities made by the investors of one country in the Bourses of another.

It is the natural tendency for a debtor country, as it makes economic progress, to buy up gradually the securities on which it has borrowed from others, and so to reduce or extinguish the amount that it has to provide abroad for interest payments. For example, Italian Rentes, the public debt of Italy, were formerly largely in the hands of foreign holders in France, Germany, and England. Italy's economic progress has been remarkable ever since her ambitions in the direction of colonial expansion and world-politics received a timely check on the Red Sea. Since then she has developed her internal resources with great success, and she has been assisted by the possession of an inexhaustible asset which she exports continually, or rather lets other people come and enjoy. For Italy holds the world in fee as an exporter of Beauty—beauty in scenery, beauty in atmosphere, beauty in buildings, sunshine, association, and a hundred other things, besides her art treasures, which it would be absurd to call priceless, because to think of price in connection with them would be a vulgar irrelevance. Every year an increasing number of travellers from all lands pours into Italy to see these things, bringing circular notes and other forms of drafts wherewith to pay their way; and, in order to meet these drafts and to feed the balances with their Italian agents on which they are drawn, the other countries have to send Italy goods, or services, or securities. Thus Italy has been enabled to buy up a large proportion of her own securities which were formerly held by foreign investors. Consequently, she has largely relieved herself of the drain against coupons, and her exchange has moved rapidly in her favour. So much so that travellers in Italy who have not been there for some years are astonished to find how much less valuable the English sovereign has become when measured by its exchange price in Italian currency.

These purchases of securities by the investors of one nation in the Stock Exchanges of others are a constantly fluctuating element, which has a marked effect on the balance of national indebtedness, and is extremely difficult to trace or gauge. Equally so is the perhaps still more important element provided by the shifting from one centre to another of the more highly specialized forms of securities, chief among which is the bill of exchange. And when we arrive at the ebb and flow of this restless ocean we come to the point at which the foreign exchanges most obviously affect the main subject of our inquiry, and it begins to be clear that this attempt to explain them was by no means an irrelevant infliction. For the movements of bills of exchange from one centre to another depend to a great extent on the rates of discount respectively current in them.

If the rate of discount be relatively low in London, bills will be poured in from abroad to be discounted and turned into cash here, and foreigners will use their credits here, and draw bills on London and discount them; and so our imports of securities will be increased, and the exchanges will be turned against us. And if the exchanges are against us, and gold is being taken from London, this state of affairs is remedied by a rise in the rate of discount here, which checks this import of bills and impels foreigners to remit funds to London to be employed in the purchase of bills; and if the process is continued, we begin to export securities, and thus turn the exchanges in our favour. And so we begin to see the great importance of the market rate of discount, owing to its effect on the foreign exchanges, and through them on the ease or difficulty with which our supply of gold is maintained.

We have thus arrived, through the thorny labyrinth penetrated in this chapter, at a result which may be summarized thus :—

The foreign exchanges are the expression of international indebtedness.

International indebtedness is the balance arising from the exchange between countries of goods, services, and securities. The movement of securities, especially of bills of exchange, depends largely on the discount rates current in the chief financial centres.

The discount rate has thus an important bearing on the foreign exchanges.

It has also been shown that when the foreign exchanges go to a certain point, gold will be taken from London, because, for example, it will pay better to send gold to Paris than to take only 25 *fr.* 15 *c.* for one's sovereign on 'change.

And gold is the basis of our credit system, since the notes and cheques which we use in commercial and financial transactions are all convertible on demand into gold, and cannot safely be multiplied beyond a certain point unless the stock of gold ready to meet them if asked for be increased also.

So that we are now beginning to see more clearly

the importance of the market rate of discount, and the need for its sagacious regulation.

The market rate of discount depends, on the one hand, on the supply of money, and, on the other, on the supply of bills of exchange which come forward to be turned into money. We have already examined the chief parts of the machinery which creates and handles money and bills of exchange—the banks, bill-brokers, and accepting houses—and we found that in normal times the supply of money and the level of discount rates are regulated by the banks. We are now in a position to try to understand the functions of the institution which takes control of the machinery when times are not quite normal, and regulates the supply of money and the market discount rate in order to affect the foreign exchanges when this intervention is considered necessary. This institution is the Bank of England.

CHAPTER XI

THE BANK OF ENGLAND

EVERY schoolboy knows, and most grown-up people have consequently forgotten, that the Bank of England was founded in 1694 to finance William III.'s Government. Since its foundation it has been the keeper of the national balance and the channel through which the nation has conducted its financial operations.

Its notes are the only form of paper currency that is legal tender in England, that is to say, that has to be accepted in payment of a debt, and it is the only joint-stock bank which is allowed to issue notes in London. As we have seen, the advantages possessed by the cheque have enabled it to supplant the note as circulating currency, but the Bank's privileges in the matter of note issue undoubtedly were of great service to it in its earlier history, and were an important cause of the prestige which now makes its name a household word for stability and soundness throughout the civilized world. It may also be presumed that they were an indirect cause of the fact that now gives the Bank its source of greatest strength and importance, namely, its position as the bankers' bank.

It has already been shown that the Bank of England's privilege in the matter of note issue in London was intended to give it the monopoly of joint-stock banking in London, and that the flank of this monopoly was only turned when it was discovered that note issuing was not an essential part of banking. The result of this discovery, instead of weakening the Bank of England by the creation of a host of nimble competitors, strengthened it by providing it with a number of enterprising and wealthy customers, who developed banking facilities all over the country in a manner which would have been impossible to it, without a radical alteration in its machinery and constitution, left with it the cash balances that were not required for their till money and country reserves, and so not only increased its dignity and visible strength, but made its task of financing the Government simpler and cheaper, reducing it to a great extent to a matter of entries in its own books.

For see what happens when the Government has to pay its quarterly dividends on Consols and other Government stocks, and finds itself in need of two millions or so for this purpose. It borrows two millions from the Bank of England, and the Bank of England gives it a credit for this amount in its books, against which the Government draws its dividend warrants. But only a small fraction of this amount is actually withdrawn. For the most part the warrants are paid into the other banks to the credit of their Consols-owning customers, and are paid in by them to the Bank of England to the credit of their balances with it. So that instead of making a great provision of cash the Bank only has to set its clerks to work with their pens rather faster than usual, and the thing is done. Thus two of the principal duties of the Bank of England, its management of the Government's money matters and its custody of the other banks' balances, fit into and assist one another very aptly.

Equally simple is the Bank's still more important task of providing emergency currency, and again for the same reason, the fact of its being banker to the collective banking community. In all economically developed communities there are periods when the normal supply of cash is insufficient, as, for example, at harvest time in agricultural countries and at the ends of the quarters, when everybody has to pay his rent and meet other periodical demands, and especially in this country at the end of the two half-years, when a large number of firms and companies all over the kingdom draw up their balance-sheets and strive to show a fine proportion of cash in their assets. And at the end of the December half-year these demands coincide with a big movement of actual currency into circulation to provide for Christmas travelling and money paid over tradesmen's counters for Christmas presents and the material ingredients of Christmas jollity. Consequently, at these periods there comes a seasonal demand for what is called money, and the Bank of England, by reason of being the bankers' bank, is able to provide it with extraordinary ease and expedition.

For money in England, as we have long ago recognized, chiefly means a credit with a bank, carrying the right to draw a cheque. In so far as it means actual coin and notes, the problem here is the same as elsewhere, and the periodical withdrawals of these for the cash payments alluded to periodically affect the Bank's reserve. But the great proportion of the seasonal demands are met by cheques, and a large part of them, those arising out of the desire to show large cash holdings in balance-sheets, are for ornamental purposes, and are only wanted to impress shareholders and customers.

Hence it follows that a large proportion of the emergency currency required at the end of the quarters is created for show and not for use, and is borrowed from the Bank, not to be withdrawn or passed on, but so as to figure in balance-sheets included among "cash in hand and at the Bank of England."

We thus arrive at an important distinction between the credits given by the Bank of England and those of the other credit-making banks. When the latter make an advance against any kind of security or buy stock for investment, they create a deposit and give a right to draw a cheque, which is probably exercised; the cheque drawn transfers the customer's credit to the customer of some other bank, and, as we saw in Chapter V., the loans of one bank create the deposits of another, except when the loans are raised with one bank for repaying another. But in the case of the Bank of England, its position as the bankers' bank results in any credits that it makes for its customers being left with itself, having been transferred from one bank to another in its books; and, what is still more important, the credits that it makes rank as cash for the rest of the banking world, so that the demand for cash for ornamental purposes in balance-sheets can be satisfied with remarkable ease by book entries. And thus banking development has outwitted and eluded the well-meant effort of the Legislature to guide and regulate it.

The Bank of England's monopoly of note issue, which was intended to give it the monopoly of joint-stock banking in the metropolitan area, was nullified by the discovery that note issuing was not the most important part of banking, and yet some years after this discovery had been marked by the foundation of the joint-stock banks, which are now, collectively, the Bank of England's biggest and most important customer, the Legislature passed an Act which elaborately regulated the note issue of the Bank of England as if its note issue were still the central feature of its business and the only thing which merited the consideration of parliamentary wisdom.

It will be remembered that the Bank Charter Act of 1844, or Peel's Act, as it is sometimes called, laid down the principle that the amount of notes issued by the Bank against securities should not exceed the sum of £14,000,000, unless by the surrender of the note-issuing privilege by other banks, which exercised it, of course, outside the circle of the Bank of England's monopoly. Any more notes issued were to be based on metal held in the Bank's vaults.

The business of a bank, as the word is now understood, consists in providing currency payable in gold, and earning a profit by calculating the amount of gold that it is necessary to hold against this liability. The Bank Charter Act thus proposed to revolutionize banking by taking away from the Bank of England the right of allowing it to judge for itself of the proportion between cash and securities that it held on the assets side of its balance-sheet against the notes issued on the other. "Your securities," it said in effect, "are to remain as they are, and for every extra £5 note that you issue in future you shall hold £5 in coin or bullion."

As to what might have happened if the Act

had worked in the manner intended by its promoters, is a matter of interesting but idle speculation. Banking evolution has evaded or avoided the question by the development of a habit of regarding a credit in the books of the Bank of England as just as good as so many bank-notes or sovereigns or bars of bullion. Borrowers do not, as a rule, ask it for notes, but for a credit in its books.

By means of this system emergency currency and credit are provided with extraordinary ease. It has grown automatically, commands complete confidence, and works with a perfection that no theoretically planned scheme can rival. If the supply of money runs short, borrowers come to the Bank of England with securities of the kind that it approves, and in the course of a few minutes' conversation with the principal of the discount office add a million or two to the basis of credit as expeditiously and easily as the ordinary citizen can buy a pair of gloves. The machine is a miracle of ease and efficiency.

The result, as it appears in the published statements of the Bank's position, is merely that the Bank of England shows an increase in securities on one side of the balance-sheet—these being the securities against which it has made advances—and an increase in deposits on the other; and the popular habit of gauging the position of a bank by the amount of its deposits would lead hasty observers to the gratifying conclusion that some fresh mass of accumulated wealth had been stored up and deposited at the Bank, and that it and its customers were richer than ever. Really all that has happened is that the Bank of England has lent "money" to some more borrowers, and, being banker to the other banks, has been able to do so by making a book entry, instead of seeing the "money" taken away from it in the shape of notes or coin.

Actually, of course, the Bank of England's position has been, when strictly considered, weakened by the operation, because the increase in deposits is an increase in liabilities, and the increase in liabilities without an increase in cash necessarily means that the proportion between cash and liabilities has been lowered, and the proportion between cash and liabilities is the most obvious touchstone that is first applied to the position of a bank in considering its apparent strength. And this question of the cash brings us to the Bank of England's other most important function—that of acting as keeper of the gold reserve for the rest of the banking community.

This function, it is interesting to observe, also arises out of the fact that the Bank of England is banker to the other banks. They, by keeping their balances with it, have, as we have seen, greatly facilitated the readiness and despatch with which the Bank finances the Government and creates emergency currency; but, at the same time, they have imposed on it this heavy burden and responsibility of maintaining the ultimate reserve, and the Bank of England is never able to forget that its liabilities are not as the liabilities of other banks, since they contain that big block of bankers' balances, which the other banks regard and treat as cash, and use as the basis for the soaring structure of credit that they build up on it.

The obligation and responsibility are all the more onerous, because they have arisen, as it were, as an unsuspected irrelevance, and were long unrecognized and unacknowledged. It might have been thought that when the Bank Charter Act of 1844 had definitely laid down the duty of the Bank of England with regard to its note issue, all that it had to do was to carry out its legal responsibility with due punctuality, and, for the rest, to carry on banking business on ordinary banking lines.

This, in fact, was the view long entertained by an influential section of the Bank's Court of Directors, and its fallacy was exposed in that most brilliant of all essays in practical economics, Walter Bagehot's great work on "Lombard Street." Bagehot not only exposed the fallacy, but killed it, buried it, and damned it. To do the Bank Court justice, it should be mentioned that even those of the directors who maintained it in theory did not advocate its practice, but spoke of a 33 per cent. cash reserve as adequate, though the ordinary banks would even now regard such a proportion as extravagant. In these days, even the theory has been abandoned, and the Bank of England has so effectually recognized the gulf that separates it from other bankers that it normally shows a proportion of cash to liabilities that is roughly twice as large as that shown by those of the other banks which are strongest in that respect, and perhaps twenty times as high as that which is apparently considered adequate by the weakest. In other words, the Bank might, if it reverted to the theory that it was only one bank among many working on the same principles, double the amount of its liabilities with a corresponding increase in its investments and dividends without altering the amount of its cash.

It is true that the greater part of the Bank of England's cash reserve in the banking department consists of its own notes issued by its issue department. But these notes are secured according to the provisions of the Bank Charter Act, and the other banks, with the practice of which we are now comparing the Bank of England's, include in their cash not only Bank of England notes but credits in its books.

But Bagehot's brilliant criticism of the manner in which the Bank recognized its responsibilities was chiefly concerned with its handling of the demands brought upon it by internal crises, and in days when an internal crisis meant a demand all over the country for Bank of England notes. Since its publication the position has been modified in two important respects. In the first place, the development of the use of cheques and of book-entry credits has been so great that it may fairly be inferred that at least the early stages of an internal crisis need not have much effect in the shape of a demand for notes. It is, of course, possible, that a panic might arise in England so severe that members of the mercantile community might refuse to accept one another's cheques in payment of debts, and that we should take a temporary step backwards to the exclusive use of sovereigns and Bank of England notes. In that case the situation would have to be met by a suspension of the Bank Act in the old-fashioned style, the temporary abrogation of the limits imposed by it on the Bank's freedom of action, and the unlimited creation of notes to meet the demand. But apart from actual general cataclysm it seems reasonable to expect that any gap in credit might probably be filled by a mere enlargement of the Bank's advances, and a consequent increase in the credits which it gives to other credit-makers to serve as a basis for their operations. In other words, instead of the Bank's reserve being depleted by internal panic, it might have the effect of merely increasing its holding of securities and its liability under deposits, as normally happens at the end of the half-years.

In the second place, the problem that the Bank of England has to face is much more external than it seems to have been when Bagehot wrote. During the last thirty-five years the machinery of internal credit has worked so well and smoothly, and succeeded, in 1890, by the application of the principle of co-operative assistance, in facing a very serious difficulty with so little discomfort—when the magnitude of the possible disaster is considered—that the possibility of real internal panic is almost forgotten, and is ignored by some of our less prudent banking institutions to an extent which is perhaps a little dangerous. On the other hand, the general adoption of the gold standard by the economically developed countries of the world, accompanied by the fact that London has remained the only market in which every draft and every credit are immediately convertible into gold as a matter of course, has greatly intensified the responsibility of the Bank of England as custodian of a gold reserve, which is liable to be drawn on at any time from all quarters of the habitable globe from which a draft on London may be presented.

The difficulty of this task that it has to perform is increased, if not created, by the fact that it has, in normal times, little control over the extent to which these credits in London are granted. For here again we find that the other banks are once more ultimately responsible, just as we have seen that they are now chiefly responsible for the creation of a mass of internal credit and currency, which they build on the foundation of the Bank of England's reserve, but expand at their own discretion and at rates which have no connection or sympathy with the official rate that is named by the Bank. By the bills that they discount and lend against, by financing the bill-brokers, and by advancing against Stock Exchange securities, the other banks give foreign financiers a pull on the Bank of England's reserve, and the Bank of England is expected to maintain it. This responsibility is shared by the accepting houses, which by accepting for a foreigner, create a bill which he can discount at the Bank of England through a bill-broker, and so give him credit which he can convert into gold.

Owing to the extent to which banking facilities have been developed outside it, the Bank of England's official rate is often a quite empty formula, and the business of the London market is carried on without any relation to it; and herein is another point in which the money market of to-day differs from that described in Bagehot's "Lombard Street," for we find Bagehot constantly assuming that any change made by the Bank of England in its rate would at once affect, and be followed by, those current in the open market. "At all ordinary moments," he writes, "there is not money enough in Lombard Street to discount all the bills in

Lombard Street without taking some money from the Bank of England." This is no longer true. Nowadays the Bank, in order to make its rate effective often has to take special measures of a kind which will be described later.

At present let us recapitulate the work that the Bank of England has to do, and then briefly consider the organization by means of which it faces its responsibilities.

It keeps the balance of the British Government and manages its finance.

It keeps the balances of the other banks, which treat their credits in its books as equivalent to cash.

It provides emergency currency at seasons of stringency, by expanding its book-entry credits and so increasing the amount of this so-called cash.

It keeps a cash reserve which is relatively about double that held by those of the other banks which are strongest in this respect, and perhaps twenty times as big as those which are weakest.

It keeps the central gold reserve of the one money market in which any form of credit instrument is immediately convertible into gold, and so has to be ready for any emergency that may arise anywhere, making somebody with a credit in London determined to take away its proceeds in the shape of metal.

Its advantages and responsibilities are thus very evenly divided. Its acting as banker to the

Government gives it prestige which is invaluable, conveys the impression that it always has the Government behind it, and in fact often produces the mistaken notion that it is a State institution, instead of a company with stock-holders. And its holding of the balances of the other banks enables it to lend money to Government and to create emergency currency by a mere transfer in its books. On the other hand, since the bankers use their balances with it as cash and as the basis of the credit that they make, the Bank of England has therefore to see to it that the reserve against these balances is not exposed to the demands of too many other customers; and hence the relatively high proportion between its cash and liabilities, which tells heavily on its power to earn dividends. This obligation of maintaining a relatively big cash reserve is increased in intensity, and made more difficult in execution, by the fact that the Bank of England holds the central gold stock of the one free market in gold in the world, and has to be prepared to meet at any moment demands on it that may come forward from abroad, and have been rendered possible by credits given by its credit-making customers, or created by accepting houses in the shape of bills discounted with it through a bill-broker.

Having thus reviewed the Bank of England's responsibilities and privileges, difficulties and advantages, let us see what kind of machinery and organization it brings to bear on its problems.

It is like no other bank in the world, and its eccentricities begin before you have crossed its threshold. Its external appearance, which its inhabitants and frequenters take as a matter of course, makes the country visitor gape with wide-mouthed wonder; one of them, on learning to his surprise that it was not Newgate Gaol, accounted for his error by saying that he thought it must be a prison because it had not any windows. Except where pierced by windows over the main entrance, the Bank's external walls are all solid, but of course it is part of its business to be among other things a fortress, capable of resisting physical attack by needy gentlemen too eager in the interests of the better distribution of wealth. It has done so before now, as every one knows, because the story of the Gordon Riots is told not only in history books but in "Barnaby Rudge." Even more obvious and impressive is the low level of its roof, and the fact that this big block of space in a spot where ground is worth so much a foot is covered by a building most of which consists of vaults and two stories. An enterprising American, viewing sadly this waste of an invaluable site, remarked that if that old bank had a live president, he would run up twenty floors on the top of it, make ten times its dividends as a real estate company, and not bother any more about the mouldy old banking business.

Internally it boasts spacious courtyards and a garden full of brilliant bloom and green leaves, in seasons when such things are possible, making a most effective and restful contrast with the grim grey walls, the roar of traffic outside, and the jingle of gold that can be heard occasionally from the big hall in which notes are being cashed. It also contains a certain amount of consecrated ground, part of its site being an old churchyard. Hence it was that an unfortunate giant, who was also a clerk in the Bank, fearing that his seven feet of skeleton would be too valuable a prey for the body-snatchers to miss, got himself buried within the Bank's walls in the vain hope that his bones might there rest in peace. Not many years ago some workmen making alterations in the vaults came on a gigantic human jaw-bone; it was sold to a dentist, who proudly exhibits it to patients, and so the giant's fears have been partially realized.*

When we come to consider the Bank's organization, its most striking features are the constitution of its Court of Directors, and its system of government by rotation, and these are points on which the Bank's critics have fastened with the keenest energy and determination.

The Bank Court is a committee recruited chiefly

* F. Straker, "The Money Market," ch. ii.

from the ranks of the accepting houses and merchant firms, and its members are nominated by itself, subject to the purely formal confirmation of the shareholders; and it is an unwritten law that no banker in the ordinary sense of the word, that is, no one connected with what we call the cheque-paying banks, can be a member of it.

At first sight this is one of those anomalous absurdities so common in England, and so puzzling to the intelligent foreigner, who cannot understand why we suffer them. A Court of Directors ruling the Bank of England, and so performing most important banking functions, and yet disqualifying for membership any one with an expert knowledge of banking, is a tempting subject for an epigrammatically minded satirist. But in fact this anomaly, like many of our others, not only works excellently well in practice, but is, when calmly considered, clearly based on sound common-sense. For in the first place it would obviously be undesirable that a member of one of the outer ring of banks should have the insight into the position of his rivals which membership of the Bank of England Court would give him, unless all the others were similarly privileged. But if all the outer banks were represented on the Bank Court, it would become a committee of unwieldy dimensions, perhaps reproducing or reflecting in the Bank parlour the rivalries and jealousies that stimulate the outer banks to work against one another, but are not conducive to their working together. And the question of proportionate representation would be difficult to settle. As it is, the Bank Court, being free from connection with the outer banks except by keeping their balances, is able to watch their proceedings with a wholly impartial eye, and, on occasion, to make suggestions with salutary effect.

Moreover, the functions, already described, that are performed by the Bank of England, are obviously different in many important respects from those fulfilled by the outer banks. Its chief customers, the Government and the other banks, are so special in kind that the custody of their funds has to be approached from a special point of view, and the Bank's duty of maintaining the gold reserve by regulating the ebb and flow of the international bullion stream is a problem for which the ordinary banker's training would be of little assistance, and for which the Bank's directors are obviously better qualified, owing to the closer touch with business affairs abroad, which arises from their connection with the accepting houses and merchant firms.

Nevertheless the narrowness of choice that limits the Bank Court in selecting its new members is certainly one of the drawbacks of its organization, and its difficulty in finding fit recruits tends to increase owing to the changing conditions of modern business. Some widening in the sweep of its net seems to be desirable, and will doubtless be brought about by the alertness that the Bank has shown in recent years in adapting itself to alterations in its environment. As an example of this alertness it may be mentioned that the Bank was one of the first institutions in the City to adopt female clerical labour on a considerable scale.

More genuine are the objections to the rotatory system, by which the Governor of the Bank holds office for two years, having previously served for two years as Deputy Governor, and then—so say the critics of the system,—just at the time when he has mastered his duties, retires into the obscurity of the Committee of Treasury, which is composed of members of the Court who have "passed the chair." Apart from the objection already noted, one result of this system is that a Bank director is not likely to become Governor until he has been many years a member of the Court. Consequently the new members of the Court have to be chosen when young, in the hope that in twenty years or so they may be capable Governors, and this is sometimes a matter of perilous hazard.

It cannot be denied that the system by which the Governor is put into the chair is somewhat haphazard. Nevertheless, it has its advantages. The Committee of Treasury represents a body of experience which is always at the Governor's service, and the periodic tenure of office makes the Governor more inclined to lean on the experience and suggestions of his colleagues on the Court, and of the heads of the various departments, and to be less a self-sufficing autocrat than he would probably become if he held office permanently, as is often proposed. And it is very important that the ruler of the Bank of England should be amenable to, and express, the broad common-sense of the commercial community as a whole, and not the prejudices and convictions of any individual, however gifted. But it is not the purpose of this work to enumerate and examine the many proposals that have been made for improving the constitution of the Bank of England. Subjected to the test of results, it shows a record that is not only unrivalled, but unapproached. For no other institution in the world attempts even to face the problem of being always ready to carry out the immediate conversion of any draft on the centre of which it is the head, which is cheerfully and composedly undertaken by the Bank of England. The elasticity of the English system, which works with the Bank as its centre, is the envy of the world, and any alteration, however slight, in so delicate a machine as a credit system, might have effects which were not at all intended.

The Bank of France is frequently pointed to as the ideal exponent of international banking by those whose test of the merits of a bank is the infrequency of the movements in its official rate. This view naturally appeals to Chambers of Commerce and the mercantile community, which chiefly desires to have its money first of all cheap, and secondly, steady in price. But the cause which keeps the official rate of the Bank of France so steady is the fact that the Bank of France is not faced by the problem involved by banking business as we understand it, namely, the immediate meeting of liabilities in gold. France still cherishes relics of Bi-metallism, and its Bank is consequently able to please itself as to whether it will meet its notes in gold or silver. Seated behind this comfortable rampart, which protects him from most of the shocks that banking flesh is heir to, the Governor of the Bank of France can maintain the most dignified steadiness in his rate, knowing that if too many claims are presented on him, he can tender payment for them in five-franc pieces, mere token counters whose bullion value is less than half the price at which he can, by the law of France, hand them to creditors in payment of claims. He is thus enabled to refuse to part with gold except as and when he pleases. It is a delightful position, but it is not banking, as we understand it, and it has its limitations; at times of crisis even the Bank of France is unable to ignore altogether what is happening in the outside world, which is wanting to turn securities and commodities into gold.

In the last quarter of 1907, for example, when the American crisis threw an exceptional strain on the world's money market, the Bank of England faced the position with cool-headed readiness, and was prepared to meet all demands on it from America, and to reinforce itself by putting its rate up and drawing in gold from other centres. The determination which it showed finally compelled the Bank of France to take some share in the international burden and to send three millions of its gold, not to America but to London, whence it knew that it could rely on getting it back. It has been commonly stated that the Bank of England asked it to carry out this operation, but this is quite untrue. The whole arrangement was made outside the Bank of England, which approved of but by no means asked for it. The Bank of France made an excellent and profitable investment in sterling bills, and helped to mitigate a storm which threatened the French monetary community with unpleasant consequences. And at the same time it was enabled to pose very gracefully as fairy godmother to the world at large, and superficial observers cried out that there must be something in its management that enabled it to play this pretty part. If the Bank of England had the right to meet its liabilities in five-shilling pieces containing half a crown's worth of silver, it might perform with equal brilliance; but then the whole of the very profitable exchange and banking business which is based on the immediate convertibility into gold of the draft on London, would be an impossibility. Under these circumstances it might be quite easy to keep the Bank of England's rate as steady as that of the Bank of France. But Bank rate has not yet been explained, and it, and its relations to the market rate, will require a fresh chapter.

CHAPTER XII

BANK RATE AND MARKET RATE

BANK rate is the official *minimum* rate at which the Bank of England will discount bills. It differs from the market rate of discount in that it is normally higher, and in that it is not a constantly fluctuating rate, shifting with the supply of and demand for bills, but is fixed and announced every Thursday morning at a special meeting of the Bank Court, and except under most unusual circumstances is not changed on any other day. But the fact that it is only the *minimum* is occasionally enforced in practice, if the Bank finds that too many bills are being brought to it for discount; on such occasions it sometimes refuses to take bills except at a higher rate, which usually becomes the official rate on the following Thursday. For loans and advances the Bank usually charges half per cent. more than for discounting bills. When the Bank is discounting bills at the official rate, or making advances at or above it, Bank rate is said to be effective, because the Bank is then in a position to regulate, more or less, the price of money in London.

It should be noted that the official rate only rules at its head office, and there only partially. The Bank of England discounts at the market rate for private customers at its head office and also at its branches; in fact, according to the frequent complaints of the other banks, it competes with them in the country by under-cutting in the matter of rates in a manner which annoys them seriously, and with some reason. Here again the Bank has been elbowed into a very difficult position by the force of circumstances. Its branches were never a spontaneous creation, but were founded by it largely in answer to a demand for them in the country which arose out of special and temporary conditions; now that the industrial and agricultural centres have been enmeshed in a network of banking facilities, the branches of the Bank of England remain, and necessarily make some exertion to justify their existence. Hence very natural grumbling on the part of the other banks, which say that the Bank of England takes their money and uses it to underbid them in their own territories.

This grievance against the Bank of England brings into view at once an important quality of the official Bank rate, namely, the fact that it is, in normal times, seldom effective. If the Bank then wants discount business, it has to take bills at a lower rate. If it took bills in the country only at its official rate its customers, the other banks, would have no genuine cause of complaint, and the Bank would get few bills, if any; but when it steps off its pedestal and enters into the chaffering circle of the market, and chaffers against the market with the market's money, the market has reason to feel that it has a grievance.

This want of connection between the official rate and the market rate also has the effect of leaving the market rate wholly without regulation. The market rate, as has already been shown, is at most times practically arrived at by competition among the other banks and higgling between them, the bill-brokers and the sellers of the bills; and hence it follows that it is ruled by mere hap-hazard cross-currents of individual conceptions on the subject of any particular business proposition that may come forward, and is not directed by the guidance of any consideration for the welfare of the market and of the monetary world as a whole. An individual banker or bill-broker who wants to add to his holding of bills or renew his maturities naturally discounts at the best rate he can get, and cannot be expected to stop and wonder whether his purchase at a lower rate of discount will have an adverse effect on the foreign exchanges, or give some foreign financier too close a hold on London's store of gold. Hence it often happens that we read in the money articles of the newspapers remarks expressing regret concerning the rapidity with which rates are being allowed to decline, as if the bankers and bill-brokers were carrying out some questionable and immoral transaction, when all that they are doing is to buy the bills that they want at the only rate at which the conditions allow them to do so: and it must seem strange that City editors should shake their heads so sadly about the behaviour of the discount market, while they accept a rise or fall in Consols as due to the inevitable action and reaction of supply and demand in the stock market.

The justification for this attitude towards the movements of the discount market arises out of the very close connection which we have already seen to exist between the market rate of discount and the foreign exchanges. When the market rate of discount is allowed to fall relatively low in London, bills of exchange are naturally sent here in increasing numbers from foreign countries to be discounted; that is to say, our imports of securities are stimulated, and so the balance of international indebtedness is affected, we have more payments to make abroad, and the rates of exchange tend to move towards the point at which it pays better to ship gold than to buy drafts. The London rate is normally low when compared with those of other centres; but the extent of its relative lowness is a question of degree; and when this degree becomes exaggerated in a manner which the general monetary outlook does not seem to justify, a situation arises which occasionally calls for deprecating comment by the Press, which endeavours to reflect the judicious opinion of the City. The individual bankers and brokers, however, whose competition depresses discount rates, are little deterred by these considerations; in the first place, because each one would think it absurd to suppose that his individual action would have any appreciable effect; in the second, because even if it had, he would consider that he could not be expected to refuse a fine parcel of bills in order that by holding out for a higher rate he might prevent an adverse movement in the exchanges. Adverse exchanges make them cautious in their purchases of bills in their own interests, because adverse exchanges generally hold out a promise of higher rates, and so encourage buyers to wait. But individual buyers cannot be expected to be deterred by consideration for the interests of the market as a whole.

So once again we arrive at the fact that the store of gold which the Bank of England is expected to keep is constantly threatened by a mass of credit created by the other banks, which work without any immediate reference to the Bank of England's position, but to suit the requirements of their own business. And thus the beautiful elasticity of our monetary system leads to a certain lack of cohesion, which requires, occasionally, drastic measures by the Bank of England to correct it.

This lack of cohesion is a comparatively modern development, and has arisen out of the great growth of the credit-making machinery which is outside of the Bank of England, but is loosely founded on its reserve, and renders its reserve liable to attack by every credit given to a foreigner, by means of a discount or an advance. In Bagehot's time the power of the Bank of England was evidently much more easily exercised, and we find him stating, in the passage quoted on page 211, that in normal times Lombard Street could not discount its bills without the help of money provided by the Bank. In other words, when he wrote, Bank rate was always effective, save on exceptional occasions.

So far is this now from being so, that in order to make its rate effective, the Bank of England often has to borrow money that it does not want, because, the market supply of money being abundant, it knows that the bankers and brokers will continue to discount bills at rates which will keep the foreign exchanges against us, unless a curtailment of the supply of money is carried out. In other words, the credit-making machinery has worked so efficiently in the output of its product that the Bank of England, which has to be ready to meet the liabilities so created, has to take some of the output away from its holders, and pay them a rate for restricting their temptations to take bills at too low rates.

This it does by going into the money market and borrowing. Any money that it borrows can only be got back from it by being borrowed again, and it, of course, only lends, at its head office, at the official rate, or ½ per cent. above it.

It has already been observed that when the Bank of England lends money the result of the operation is generally expressed in a book entry, by which it shows more securities (which it has received as collateral) among its assets, and more deposits among its liabilities. When it borrows, the book entry of course works similarly, but contrariwise; its holding of securities is reduced by the fact that part of them is pledged to the lenders, and the amount that it borrows cancels so much of its liability under deposits, in other words, reduces the balances of the other banks, and so narrows the basis of credit, makes money dear, brings the market rate of discount into some connection with the official rate, influences the foreign exchanges, and increases the probability that gold will be sent to London, or that gold which arrives will not be taken for export. By this roundabout process the Bank finally arrives at its object of protecting or increasing its reserve.

It has been said that by borrowing money the Bank of England reduces the balances of the other banks; this it does either directly by borrowing part of their balances from them, or indirectly, by borrowing from the bill-brokers and finance houses, who pay it what they lend with cheques on the banks, which to that extent cancel the balance of the banks in question at the Bank of England. The banks in question, having their balances at the Bank thus reduced, either reduce the credits that they have based on them, or more probably restore their balances by calling in money from the bill-brokers, their loans to whom have already been described as their second line of defence, after their holding of cash in hand and at the Bank of England. The bill-brokers, from whom these loans are called in, first have recourse to the other bankers and money-lenders, trying to fill the gap that has been made in the funds on which they work their business, but are finally, as it generally happens, driven to the Bank of England, whence they have to borrow part of the money that it has borrowed from the market, and will have to pay for it at or over the official rate, which is thus made effective, and becomes a controlling factor in market rates. The system is thus clumsy and artificial, and, as has been observed, is comparatively novel, having been brought into existence by the great development of the activities of the other banks, which have manufactured credit so successfully that part of the output has sometimes to be absorbed by the

Bank of England, which does not want it, but has to prevent the evil consequences that might result from its over abundance.

The bill-brokers, whom we have seen to be the first sufferers when the Bank of England thinks it necessary to reduce the overgrown mass of credit, generally wax eloquent concerning the absurdities of the system, the hardship involved to all legitimate users of credit when it is thus artificially controlled, and the monstrous interference with the natural laws of supply and demand, which ought, they contend, to be left to regulate the value of money like that of every other commodity.

Their position is certainly one with which a disinterested observer can readily sympathize, for they are constantly tempted, not to say forced, by the free credit facilities given by the other banks, into taking bills at rates which have an adverse effect on the foreign exchanges; and then the Bank of England, in order to rectify the position, has to reduce the mass of credit, and the bill-brokers find themselves, with their portfolios full of bills taken at low rates, artificially deprived of the wherewithal to carry them, and obliged to pay an unexpectedly high price for money to finance their bills, or rediscount them with the Bank of England at a loss.

Nevertheless their appeal to economic first principles, and the natural laws of supply and demand, does not seem to bear examination. Even in the production of agricultural and industrial commodities the law of supply and demand, if left unfettered, brings many evils in its train, the most obvious among which are the periodical spells of exuberance and depression to which the producing industries are habitually exposed, to their own loss and that of the community as a whole. For some time past the civilized world has submitted to these evils as inevitable or as small in comparison with the great benefit arising from the increase in production that has taken place under the system of unrestricted competition; but there are very plain indications that this acquiescent attitude is being modified. The modern trend of production is certainly in the direction of co-ordination, co-operation, combination, and regulation, and unrestricted competition seems to be gradually retiring into the obscurity of obsolescence.

But in this matter of the supply of credit and of credit instruments it has long been recognized that regulation is essential, and that the free play of supply and demand cannot be left to itself, because of the vast and wide-spreading disasters that result to the whole of a community from any dislocation in the machinery of credit. Moreover, it must be remembered that supply and demand cannot possibly work as effectively in the case of money as in that of an ordinary commodity, because of an important and essential difference which sets a great gulf between money, in the modern English sense, and concrete and tangible commodities. This difference lies in the fact that the cost of production of money is a negligible factor in its price. If the farmer is bid £1000 for his crop, his answer will be strongly influenced by the amount of work and capital that have been spent on producing it, and will be required for producing another; when a banker is bid 4 per cent. for a loan of £1000 for six months, in other words, is offered £1020 six months hence for £1000 to-day, the sum that it will have cost him or somebody else to produce that £1000 will hardly enter into his calculation; for it will be merely a matter of cheque drawing and book entries involving a certain amount of penmanship, and whether the loan is for £1000 or £1,000,000 will make little difference—very likely none at all—to the cost involved to the producer of it. It was quite otherwise when money consisted of metal that had to be dug out and treated; but now that money is a matter of book entries and pieces of paper, which pass current because they are convertible into gold and so have to have a certain amount of gold behind them—but are brought into being according to the varying views of bankers, as to how much may safely be based on a given quantity of gold—the supply of money can obviously be multiplied without any question of cost, so long as borrowers have security to offer, and bankers are prepared to make book entries.

Regulation is in fact already an accepted part of our monetary system, and we have seen that the Bank Charter Act carefully and precisely regulated the number of bank-notes that might be created. If the bank-note had retained its position as the most important of our credit instruments, Bank rate would have retained its control of the money market, that is to say, the rate at which the Bank of England was prepared to provide borrowers with notes would have remained the dominant factor in the price of money. But we have seen that the regulation arranged by the Bank Act has been set aside by the development of the use of cheques, and the dominant factor in the price of money is now the rate at which the other banks are prepared to provide borrowers with the right to draw cheques.

Hence it is that the Bank of England, which is expected to keep a gold reserve for the whole economic body, English and foreign, whence any one who has a cheque on England can help himself at a moment's notice, is only in exceptional circumstances able to regulate the supply of credit which is based on its reserve.

These exceptional circumstances arise (1) when trade is so active that the lending power of the other banks has reached its limit, and so any more credit required has to be provided by the Bank of England, at its price, and so Bank rate is effective; (2) when the payment of the direct taxes in the January to

March quarter sweeps millions into the Treasury's account at the Bank of England, which thus obtains control of the position; (3) at the end of the quarters, when the demand for credit and currency generally exceeds the outside supply, and the Bank of England has to fill the gap on its own terms; and (4) when the Bank of England decides that the conditions of the international money market make regulation imperative, and so borrows money that it does not want in order to curtail the mass of credit created by the other banks, and force discount rates up to a point at which they will have the desired effect on the foreign exchanges.

In times of crisis or of strong external demand for gold it need not be said that the Bank of England holds control either because it has taken measures to get it, or because the demand for credit has reached the limit of the outside supply, or the exports of gold have narrowed the basis of the outside supply. The weak point in the system is that in ordinary times, and especially when the price of money is declining, the Bank has no control of the position; the credit factory of the other banks works away merrily and unregulated, probably rather too fast, and perhaps laying up trouble for the next spell of depression; and in the meantime the Bank's task of increasing its reserve with a view to this next spell of depression is rendered difficult or impossible, because it has no voice in the value of money, which regulates the discount rate, which rules the exchanges.

An interesting example of the working of this weakness in our system was afforded in this summer of 1908. Every one who has followed the recent events of monetary history, knows that for some years the abnormal activity of trade and other influences had caused chronic monetary stringency, which culminated in the American crisis of 1907. This eruption effectively checked the abnormal activity of trade, and monetary stringency gave place to abundance. The Bank of England, which had stood in the breach in defence of the economic world during the crisis, and by raising its rate had drawn in gold from seventeen different countries to supply America's needs, led the way in recognizing the change in the position, and reduced its rate rapidly from 7 to 2½ per cent. during the spring of 1908, thus allowing other centres, whose reserves had been depleted during the crisis, to replenish them out of the gold which arrives regularly in London from South Africa and elsewhere. This was the obviously wise and sensible policy, but after it had been carried out it might have been thought that the next step was to set about securing that increase in the Bank's gold store which had long been urged as desirable, and was then rendered possible by the great change that had come over the money market's position.

Whether the Bank Court did or did not desire to do so, is known only to itself; it may have had information which led it to believe that monetary prospects promised continued ease, and that there was no need to regret the course of events. But the point to be noted is that even if the Bank had wished to increase its gold store, it would have been impossible for it to do so, unless it had intervened and borrowed a very large amount from the market; and this is a weapon of which it naturally only makes use when the outlook makes its employment imperative.

Bank rate was still 2½ per cent., but it was wholly ineffective and an empty symbol. The market rate was of course the rate at which the business was done, and its low level had the inevitable effect of sending a mass of bills to be discounted here, and of preventing foreign holders of English bills from renewing them as they fell due, much less increasing their purchases of them. And so England's imports of securities were stimulated to a point at which it had to send gold continually to the Continent, instead of using it to build up the reserve.

And this happened largely owing to the want of connection, in times of monetary ease, between the official rate and the market rate. The only connection that exists between them arises because the rate which bankers allow to depositors is more or less regulated by Bank rate, and is usually 1½ per cent. below it. It might be supposed that this connection would suffice to establish some relation between the Bank rate and the market rate of discount, because it would be natural to infer that the bankers would expect to make some profit between their depositors and their borrowers; if that were so it would follow that the rate at which they would lend to the bill-brokers could not fall much lower than 1 per cent. below Bank rate, and that the market discount rate would thus be kept more or less approximately in touch with the official rate. But this expectation is not borne out in practice, because the large amounts of credit * that the banks handle, besides those which are represented by sums definitely placed on deposit, make the deposit rate a factor in part only of their business. The principle on which they seem to work is the theory that it is better to get some sort of rate than none, and each one considers that if it refuses to lend to the bill-brokers at the rates which are supposed to be current, its neighbours will only get all the more business; and so in times of monetary ease, competition and rivalry deliver the bankers into the hands of the bill-brokers, who get money out of them on merely nominal terms, and then proceed to discount bills at rates which are unwholesome for the foreign exchanges.

So, to return to our example, the system

* P. 124.

worked in July, 1908, when Bank rate was $2\frac{1}{2}$ per cent., the rate allowed by bankers to depositors was 1 per cent., the rate at which bankers were lending to bill-brokers was 1 per cent., the market rate of discount was $1\frac{3}{16}$ per cent., the foreign exchanges were adverse, and all the gold that came into London from the mines of Johannesburg, went on to Paris or Berlin. It went to Paris because the low level of discount rate here made it unprofitable for French banks to renew the English bills that they held, and so gold went to pay for them as they were presented, and it went to Berlin because the low level of discount rates here enabled Berlin to pour bills—much of them mere finance paper—into this market to be discounted, and gold went to pay for these imported securities.

We thus see in this example the direct chain of causation between the competition and rivalry among the banks, which incite them to lend money to bill-brokers at, or sometimes below, the rate at which they borrow it from depositors, and the consequent inability of the Bank of England to increase its reserve, because the operations of the other banks drive gold abroad. This result of their competition and rivalry, besides being injurious to the wider interests of the money market, is unprofitable to the banks. If we could for a moment imagine that they could lay aside their rivalries and make a mutual arrangement by which they agreed not to lend money to bill-brokers or anybody else at a lower rate than $\frac{1}{2}$ per cent. above that which they are giving to their depositors, it is probable that the amount that they would lend would be reduced; but, on the other hand, the rate that they would receive on the sums lent would be very materially increased.

The result would be that they would make less credit in times of ease, and in times of ease the superfluity of manufactured credit is a dangerous temptation to speculators and kite-flyers—so much so that it has been observed by a seasoned and exceptionally well-placed watcher of the money market that "bad debts are made when money is cheap"; the banks' proportion of cash to liabilities would be higher, and their position would be stronger; their profits would be greater or no less, and the connecting link between Bank rate and the market rate would be established to an extent which would still permit of all desirable elasticity, but would provide a minimum beyond which the divorce between the two would probably not be stretched. For the market rate of discount, as has been shown, depends to a considerable extent on the current rate for loans from the banks to the bill-brokers.

Whether such an agreement is possible is another question. But the fact that a considerable number of the banks already work by mutual agreement in deciding on the rate at which they will lend money to their Stock Exchange clients is in favour of the possibility. And since the bankers already to some extent regulate the rate that they allow to depositors by Bank rate, such an arrangement as is here suggested would introduce no new principle and effect no revolution, but merely carry the application of an established principle a step further.

It would bring the Bank rate and the market rate into touch, yet quite distantly and elastically, and without establishing any cast-iron link between them. And it would enable Bank rate to work, not as now, with the assistance of artificial and expensive measures that have suddenly to be decided on and executed by the Bank of England, and upset calculations, and cause inconvenience and irritation, but by a continuous and normal relation between it and the lowest price at which credit is available in the market.

Under such circumstances the other banks might fairly claim to have a more definite influence on the movements in Bank rate; and any process which would lead to closer co-operation between them and the Bank of England would be a gain.

CHAPTER XIII

THE BANK RETURN

The account issued every Thursday by the Bank of England, giving a statement of its position, is generally regarded as the key to the condition of the London money market as a whole and is so awaited and examined with keen interest. Much ingenuity is often required in unravelling the meaning of the movements in the various items, for the return, which is drawn up in accordance with the requirements of the Bank Charter Act, is by no means a model of lucidity. And some attempt at comprehension of the return is so essential to those who wish to grope their way through the mysteries of the money market, that we must now try to arrive at some sort of distant acquaintance with it. Further than that we need not expect to go. It may be said of all balance-sheets that they are useful as a general indication, but apt to be misleading if used as a basis of detailed inferences, except by those who can go behind the figures and find out what they really mean. In the case of the Bank return, which may be said to be a balance-sheet of a kind, only the broadest and most guarded deductions are possible, and they should be accepted with caution. Parliamentary wisdom, expressed in the Bank Act, decreed that the note-issuing business of the Bank should be separated from its banking business, and that this separation should be shown in its weekly account, which gives two separate statements, one showing the position of the Issue Department, the other that of the Banking Department. It has frequently been suggested that this distinction is unreal and only darkens counsel, and that the Bank return would be clearer and simpler if the two statements were put together. There is something to be said for this view, but perhaps hardly enough to justify an alteration which would change the face of the return so completely and confuse comparisons with its predecessors of the past sixty odd years. Overleaf is a specimen of the account as now presented. Its figures are influenced by its being the last return of a half-year, so that the Other Deposits and Other Securities are increased by the Bank's provision of emergency credit. But it will serve as an illustration :—

BANK OF ENGLAND.

AN ACCOUNT pursuant to the Act 7 and 8 VICT. cap. 32, for the week ending on Wednesday, the 1st day of July, 1908.

ISSUE DEPARTMENT.

	£		£
Notes Issued ..	55,484,385	Government Debt	11,015,100
		Other Securities ..	7,434,900
		Gold Coin & Bullion	37,034,385
		Silver Bullion ..	
	£55,484,385		£55,484,385

Dated the 2nd day of July, 1908.

J. G. NAIRNE, *Chief Cashier.*

BANKING DEPARTMENT.

	£		£
Proprietors' Capital	14,553,000	Government Securities	15,231,766
Rest	3,214,385	Other Securities ..	36,347,819
Public Deposits—(including Exchequer, Savings Banks, Commissioners of National Debt, and Dividend Accounts)	9,648,021	Notes	25,508,120
Other Deposits ..	51,197,083	Gold and Silver Coin	1,573,008
Seven-Day and other Bills ..	48,244		
	£78,660,713		£78,660,713

Dated the 2nd day of July, 1908.

J. G. NAIRNE, *Chief Cashier.*

On the left or debit side of the statement of the Issue Department we find one item, that of its notes issued and outstanding, and it must be carefully observed that their amount is not that of the Bank's note circulation, because a large proportion is retained among the assets of the Banking Department, and constitutes most of what is generally called the Bank's reserve. The Bank's note circulation is arrived at by subtracting the notes held by the Banking Department from those issued by the Issue Department, by which process we arrive at the number of notes that are circulating at home and abroad or are held by the other banks to meet daily demands for cash.

On the other side of the dividing line that separates the assets and liabilities of the Issue Department appear the items on which the bank-notes are secured. First comes the Government debt, swollen to over 11 millions from the £1,200,000 to advance which to Dutch William the Bank was originally founded; this is not represented by any holding of stock, but is a book entry between the Government and the Bank, and this item should be noted, because one of the suggestions made for the creation of bigger gold reserves advocates that the Government should pay this debt to the Bank in gold and that the Bank's fiduciary note issue should thus be permanently reduced. The fiduciary (confidential) issue is that part of the issue that is based not on gold but on this Government debt and the next item, Other Securities, which consist of British Government stocks; these two aggregate nearly 18½ millions, and this figure is at present the limit up to which the Bank is allowed to issue notes against securities. It was arrived at by the provision in the Bank Act which fixed the fiduciary issue at 14 millions, and arranged that the Bank should be permitted to take over two-thirds of the authorized powers of any country bank which thereafter might allow its note issue to lapse. By means of these lapses, which arose chiefly owing to the absorption of country banks by companies which had London offices and therefore were debarred from note issuing by the Bank of England's monopoly, the fiduciary issue has grown from the 14 millions at which it was fixed by the Bank Act to the 18½ millions now shown.

Above this limit every note must have a bullion basis, and is as a matter of practice invariably based on gold. The Bank Act, however, allows one-fifth of the metallic basis of the note issue to consist of silver, and the weekly account as published by the Bank of England regularly contains the line "Silver coin and bullion" with a blank opposite to it. This power possessed by the Bank of basing part of its note issue on silver is often forgotten, but its existence was brought home to the City in 1897 when the Chancellor of the Exchequer and the

Governor of the Bank seriously discussed a proposal for putting it into practice. The arrangement was evidently due to pressure brought to bear on the Government of the day by the Bimetallists, who believed that silver and gold could be made to circulate on equal terms at a fixed ratio, to the benefit of all concerned, and this mooted concession on the part of the Bank of England was part of a scheme for improving the position of silver. But it was nipped in the bud very early in its history. The *Times* found out what was afoot and exposed the scheme with dramatic effect. There was such an outcry in the City that no more was heard of the project, and gold remains the sole basis of every note that is issued by the Bank above the 18½ million limit.

Proceeding to the Banking Department, the first item that we see on the liabilities side is the proprietors' capital, which speaks for itself, being obviously the amount subscribed by the original stockholders of the Bank, with subsequent additions. It differs from the capital of the other English banks by being in stock instead of shares, and by being fully paid up, whereas it is now the fashion for banks to have a reserve in the shape of a liability on their shareholders for uncalled capital. But though the stock of the Bank of England is fully paid, authorities differ as to whether there is further liability on it. It is not a practical question, however, or one that need keep proprietors of Bank stock awake at night, and Parliament has distinguished the stock by including it among the investments open to trustees.

The next item is the Rest, under which quaint name the Bank holds what most other banks and companies, which are fortunate enough to possess one, call a reserve. That is, it is an accumulation of profits which have not been distributed as dividends but kept in hand to strengthen the Bank's position. It may seem at first sight puzzling that the possession of a liability should strengthen a company's position, but this liability, like the subscribed capital, is a liability only between the Bank and its shareholders, and is, of course, represented by assets on the other side of the account, so that the proportion of assets to real outside liabilities—the demands that the Bank's customers can make on it—is strengthened by its existence. Unlike the reserve of an ordinary bank or company, however, the Bank of England's Rest constantly fluctuates, and it may be supposed that it more or less contains the Bank's profit and loss account balance. But it is shifted about from week to week in a manner which an outside observer can note, but not understand, and apparently most of the profit and loss balance is included in the Other Deposits, which will be dealt with later, and is transferred to the Rest when it is wanted to pay dividends withal. At any rate, it is not unusual to see a large amount suddenly added to the Rest at the end of February and August when the Bank completes its half-year, and from the amount of the Rest at those dates it is possible to calculate what the distribution will be when the Bank Court assembles for the "making of a dividend." For the Rest is never allowed to fall below 3 millions, and the amount above that level at the end of the half-year is roughly the sum available for distribution. It may be noted that this three-million level of the Rest has been constant during many decades, and has not been increased in accordance with the addition to the Bank's outside liabilities. Bagehot's "Lombard Street" gives the Bank return for the last week of 1869 with the Rest just over 3 millions and the Other Deposits at 18 millions odd. At the end of June, 1908, the Rest is still just over 3 millions, and the Other Deposits are 51 millions odd.

The Public Deposits are the balances of the various departments of the British Government, which are held and administered by the Bank of England as its banker. They fluctuate according to the briskness or sluggishness of the revenue payments, and the rapidity or slowness with which the Government is making its various disbursements. A large sum is taken off them at the beginning of every quarter, when the dividends on Consols and other Government stocks are paid, and this sum is transferred to the Other Deposits, or ultimately finds its way there. The payment of the Government dividends thus tends to make money abundant, for it means that a credit at the Bank of England has been taken from the Treasury and turned into "cash in hand and at the Bank of England" in the control of the other banks, who can use it as the basis for the manufacture of more credit. On the other hand in the March quarter of the year, when we are all paying our income-tax and house-duty, the Public Deposits swell, the Other Deposits dwindle, and money becomes scarce, or "tight" in the City phrase. It is important to remember that an increase in the Public Deposits means an increase of credits over which the Bank keeps command and control, but an increase in the Other Deposits means an increase in its liabilities to the general public and in the "cash at the Bank of England" which is used, like gold or notes, as a basis for credit-making by the other banks. It thus follows that when the payment of the direct taxes in the March quarter swells the Public Deposits at the expense of the Other, by the transfer of credits from the taxpayers to the Treasury, the other banks, in order to maintain their balances at the Bank of England, have to call in funds that they have lent. They accordingly reduce their loans at call or short notice with the bill-brokers, and the latter in order to fill the gap generally have to borrow from the Bank of England and so restore the basis of credit by producing fresh supplies of cash at the Bank of England, which take the place of those which the tax-gatherer's activity has transferred from the banks' to the Government's balance. The bill-brokers, being thus the chief sufferers from this seasonal stringency, cry out with great vigour upon the iniquities of a system which thus locks up the money of the tax-payer in the control of the Bank of England, which will only lend at a rate which is normally higher than that current in the market; and they maintain that trade is thus penalized and the clock of economic progress put back, and that it is necessary to adopt measures for a radical alteration in the whole arrangement, by which the big balance accumulated by the Treasury in the March quarter should not be retained by the Bank of England, but distributed among the other banks, which would be prepared to lend at the market rate. In all these objections there is a certain amount of reason, but they are overwhelmingly answered by the practical fact that this normal tightness of money in the March quarter gives the Bank of England a much-needed opportunity of replenishing its reserve against the demands of the latter half of the year. If the Bank rate and market rate were kept normally in closer touch there would be no need for the Bank to take advantage of the period of tax-gathering and tightness in order to strengthen itself. And then it might be possible to discuss measures for relieving this spring-tide strain on the bill-brokers, not by such revolutionary means as they are fond of suggesting, but by modifying the system under which the bulk of the direct taxes are paid in the last quarter of the financial year, and perhaps by accelerating the rapidity with which the tax-gathered money is paid out again by the Treasury. But as things are at present, the long period of control of the position which is secured to the Bank by the transfer of taxes to the Public Deposits, gives it its only chance of strengthening itself except by the adoption of borrowing measures to which it is naturally reluctant to resort.

"Other Deposits" is the comprehensive title under which the Bank includes all its liability on deposits to any one but the British Government. Within this item is locked up the secret of the real position of the money market, for it contains the balances of the other banks, and as the Other Deposits rise and fall it is fairly safe to expect that that part of the basis of credit which consists of the cash at the Bank of England which they show in their balance-sheets also expands and contracts. This expectation is fairly safe, but it must be remembered that the Other Deposits contain many other accounts besides those of the banks. It is generally believed in banking circles that the average amount of the bankers' balances is 22 to 23 millions. In the return given on page 244 they were probably swollen by the usual proceedings at the end of the half-year. But perhaps about 20 millions consisted of liabilities to other creditors, including governments, municipalities, and the Bank's many private customers. It thus follows that the really interesting movements that take place in the books of the Bank of England are hidden from the public gaze, for they are transfers to and from the various accounts which are included in the Other Deposits, and therefore do not affect their total. And hence it is that the Bank return, though in some senses a very full statement of the Bank's position, is only a tantalizing indication of the outside of things, of which monetary students crave hungrily for details.

It is often suggested that more light should be thrown on the position by the separation of the bankers' balances, in the weekly return, from those of the Bank of England's other customers. This demand for more light is attractive, but extreme caution is desirable in approaching this very delicate question. In the first place, it may be observed that no other bank makes any distinction in its balance-sheet between the various classes of its customers, so that the Bank of England by separating the Public and Other Deposits makes a certain concession to the peculiarities of its position. It is also clear that the Bank of England could not fairly be asked to give a separate statement of the balances of its banking customers unless they themselves expressed a definite and unanimous desire that it should do so. As their banker it is their confidential servant, and it has no right to tell the general public what they have got in its books, singly or collectively, unless under instructions from them.

It appears, however, that the outside bankers are, more or less at least, in favour of the separate statement of their balances. It has been advocated by an eminent chairman of a great bank in a presidential address to the Bankers' Institute, and if the request were made unanimously, it is difficult to see how the Bank of England could refuse it. The Bank of England, however, is believed to deprecate the suggestion. In former days a return was regularly moved for in Parliament showing the amount of the bankers' balances in the Other Deposits, and though the return was inevitably tardy, and only showed how matters had stood at a previous date, it was at any rate a rough indication. A revival of this practice was recently attempted, but when the return was moved for again in Parliament the motion was blocked by the Treasury, presumably at the instigation of the Bank of England. The Bank's objection to the separate publication of the bankers' balances is believed to be based on the view that if at any time its reserve were to fall below the amount due to the bankers, an unfavourable and perhaps dangerous impression might be created. It is easy to answer that the reserve ought not to be allowed to fall below the amount due to the bankers, but this reply is not wholly convincing, for elasticity and adaptability to the conditions of the moment are the most essential of all essentials in dealing with periods of monetary discomfort.

The little item of a few thousand pounds'-worth of seven-day and other bills—"a trifle, some tenpenny matter," as Prince Hal says—represents an old-fashioned form of remittance still used for certain revenue payments.

We now turn to the other side of the account to consider the assets which the Bank holds against these liabilities to its stockholders and customers. We have seen that the two first liabilities, capital and Rest, are owed by it only to its proprietors, and are therefore not a debt in the same sense as the others, and, when working out the proportion of cash to liabilities, it is only the liability to customers, the Government and other depositors, and the holders of seven-day and other bills, that is included in the calculation.

In its treatment of the liabilities side of its account we found that the Bank to this extent gives fuller information than other banks, in that it separates the Public from the Other Deposits; but on the assets side its statement, which, be it remembered, was arranged for it by Parliament sixty odd years ago, is distinguished by obscurity. It makes no distinction between its investments, its loans and its discounts, all of which are stated under the heading of securities, these being distinguished as Government and Other. In this case again Government means only British Government, and the item Government securities covers the Bank's holding of Consols and other British Government stocks, Treasury bills, Exchequer bonds, and other short obligations of the Government, and any loans that it may have to make to the Treasury in the shape of Ways and Means or Deficiency advances, when the exigencies of "supply" or of dividend payments compel the Government to draw on its banker. As these temporary borrowing operations by the Treasury are indicated more or less by the weekly returns of public income and expenditure, published in the *Gazette*, it is possible with their assistance to get a dim glimpse of the meaning of the movements in the Government securities in the Bank return; but these Government returns are slow in appearance, inadequate in information, and obscure in expression, and any one who attempts to find his way with their help towards a comprehension of the relations between the Government and the money market is entering a path full of pitfalls. It is rather curious that the money market, which so often has to come to the assistance of the Government by subscribing to Treasury bills or otherwise, submits patiently to handing over its money to a borrower whose operations are veiled in so much mystery, and at the same time are of such great importance. Broadly, however, it may be stated that when the Government securities item rises, either the Bank has been increasing its holding of Consols or other Government obligations, funded or unfunded, or else has been making some sort of an advance to the British Government; and when it declines, it goes without saying that one of the contrary operations has taken place, that the Bank has been selling its Consols, etc., or having an advance repaid by the Government; but there is yet another possibility, for the Bank may have been borrowing from the market and giving some of its Government stocks as security. When it borrows in order to curtail the supply of credit it is usual to see a decrease in the Government securities, and sometimes in the Other Securities likewise. But it is important to remember that when the Bank lends money to the market its holding of Government securities is not thereby affected; very probably it lends on the security of Consols, but this security is only collateral and the borrowers' promise to pay is what it relies on first, and it therefore includes advances to any borrower but the British Government under Other Securities.

The Other Securities are thus already to a great extent explained. They include all investments held by the Bank, other than obligations of the British Government; all advances to its private customers, or to bill-brokers, stockbrokers, municipalities, colonial Governments, accepting houses, colonial or foreign banks, or any one, except the British Government, who may have need of its services and possess the wherewithal to obtain them; all the bills that it has discounted, whether in order to provide credit for the London bill-brokers, when cash has been called in from them by the other banks, or in the ordinary course of trade. The comprehensive nature of this item thus entails much wariness in drawing conclusions from its movements, and it is often suggested that the Bank return would be a much more lucid statement of the position if its loans, discounts and investments were separately stated instead of being thus massed together. The gain in lucidity would certainly be enormous, and it is difficult to see that any valid objection can be raised against this step in the direction of publicity and clearness.

Finally, having thus arrayed the obscurities which clog any attempt to unravel the meaning of the Bank return and the movements in its various items without assistance from those who know what is behind the figures, we may arrive at the one broad and platitudinous conclusion that can invariably be drawn from a change in the Bank's holding of securities. It is safe to expect that any increase in the securities will *pro tanto* increase the supply of money, and any decrease will reduce it. For since every amount lent means a corresponding credit in the Bank's books, an increase in the securities causes a corresponding increase in the deposits, either Public or Other; and if the Public deposits have been increased by an advance from the Bank it may be assumed that this has been done because the Government has payments to make, and that the increase will shortly be transferred to the Other deposits, and so will be added to the "cash at the Bank of England" in the books of other banks, which is regarded as equivalent to gold as the basis of credit. Or the increased credit may be employed in the withdrawal of actual currency from the Bank, which will so be added to the cash in hand of the commercial community. At the same time it is equally true that an increase in the Bank's securities, though it tends to make money cheap, is generally accompanied, and caused, by dearness of money, which drives borrowers to the Bank in order to increase the supply.

And now we come to the last two items on the assets side of the account, which taken together constitute what is generally spoken of as the reserve of the Bank of England. It should be noted that this reserve is, in accordance with the confusing habit of economic phraseology, a reserve in quite a different sense from the reserve or reserve fund of another bank or company. Ordinarily a company's reserve means an accumulation from profits which have not been distributed as dividend but kept in hand for use in case of need. The Bank of England, as we have seen, possesses a reserve of this kind, and calls it its Rest. But when we speak or write of the Bank's reserve we mean its holding of cash in the Banking Department. In the account before us it consists chiefly of notes with a comparatively small proportion of coin and bullion; the coin and bullion may be called the Bank's till money, the coin that it has in hand to meet cheques drawn on it, and for other ordinary banking business. Any more gold that comes into the Bank's hands goes into the Issue Department, and notes are issued against it and put into the assets of the Banking Department. It is a confusing and complicated arrangement that makes the notes a liability of the Issue Department and an asset of the Banking Department, but we can simplify it a little by regarding the notes of which the reserve largely consists as bullion certificates representing gold in the vaults of the Issue Department.

For practical purposes we are justified in doing so, but it must not be forgotten that notes are not actually quite bullion certificates, since as we have seen they are to some extent based on securities and Government debt, and in the account before us about one-third of the backing of the notes is thus composed. And it thus appears that the liabilities of the Banking Department of the Bank of England, which are used as the basis of credit by the rest of the banking community, are represented as to one-half or rather more by securities, and as to most of the rest by notes, which are again represented as to about one-third by securities. It is a beautiful if rather complicated development of the use of credit, and economy of metal, but the attractiveness of the system, on paper, and its smooth working in practice, make it all the more essential to be sure that the solidity of the machine is carefully watched over, and that metal is not economized to a dangerous extent.

This part of the Bank of England's task is the more difficult because it has no control over the extent to which its banking customers create credit. All that it can do is to try to maintain its reserve by the use of its rate, when its rate is effective, but the quantity and quality of the credits that are given to the commercial community both local and foreign by the other bankers are matters which are necessarily in the hands of the latter. And the elasticity of the system, which is one of its chief attractions, thus results in the Bank's reserve being liable to be depleted by credits given by its customers, over which it can have no control. An advance given by one of the other banks to a foreign financier, in the shape of a loan against securities, or an acceptance or the discount of a bill, may mean that the foreigner takes advantage of the credit so given to demand gold; this demand will fall ultimately on the Bank of England, which will take the gold out of its vaults and cancel a corresponding number of notes. As it obviously cannot cancel notes in circulation it has to cancel those in its Banking Department, and so its reserve is thereby diminished by an operation of which it had no knowledge. And we so come back once more to the importance of the other banks, and see that the manner in which they conduct their business of credit-making has a very considerable bearing on the problem of the defence and maintenance of the Bank of England's reserve.

CHAPTER XIV

THE GOLD RESERVE

Having thus completed our inspection of the main wheels in the monetary machine, and arrived at a necessarily rough and elementary notion of the manner in which they work together and react upon one another, we are in a position to consider the problem that has for many years exercised the banking world, namely, the alleged inadequacy of the metallic basis on which the monetary machine manufactures credit, and the measures necessary for reinforcing it.

This inadequacy has been asserted over and over again by bank chairmen at half-yearly meetings, and by presidents of the Bankers' Institute in the course of inaugural addresses, and the few dissentients who deny its existence, generally complicate matters by maintaining that what is wrong is not the lack of gold but the over-extension of credit. We need not pause to consider this delicate subtlety. Whether the foundation be too small for the building, or the building be too big for the foundation, the same practical conclusion arises, namely, that either the building must be reduced, or the foundation must be increased, or both processes must be carried out together. And when we find bankers themselves maintaining that the gold basis of their credit operations is inadequate, it must be admitted that their evidence is of the greatest possible weight, and that any outsider who gainsaid it would incur a heavy responsibility.

We have seen that banking in England, in its modern sense, works without any legal fetter or restriction, and we have seen reason for being thankful that it does so. And we have also seen that it has perfected a marvellously efficient system of credit, with a metallic basis economized with unparallelled skill and success. And the more closely one examines the basis of credit, the more clearly it becomes apparent that that basis itself consists to a considerable extent of credit.

For example, we saw that the half-dozen big banks whose balance-sheets we amalgamated on p. 59, had as the cash basis of their liabilities on current and deposit account, which amounted to 249 millions, 43 millions of cash in hand and at the Bank of England—nearly 18 per cent., a high proportion according to present ideals. It would be interesting to know how much of this is gold. One of the banks included, the Union of London and Smith's, which we have referred to before as being conspicuously explicit in its balance-sheet, shows this same quality again by separating, alone among its peers, its cash in hand from its cash at the Bank of England. It had on June 30, 1908, £3,009,000 of cash in hand and £3,412,000 at the Bank of England. If these figures be a safe guide to the position of the Union's brethren, which we must admit that they may not be, we shall be within the mark if we assume that, out of the 43 millions held by the aggregated six, 20 millions are cash at the Bank of England, that is, are a liability of the Bank of England to these six banks. But the Bank of England's normal proportion of cash to liabilities in its Banking Department ranges from about 35 to 55 per cent.; and if we take it at 50 per cent., we are again doing full justice to the position; so that of these 20 millions on which the six banks have based credits 10 are represented by cash held by the Bank of England. Moreover, the cash held by the Bank of England's Banking Department consists chiefly of its own notes, and its notes, though regarded for practical purposes as a bullion certificate, are actually backed by securities to the extent of nearly 18½ millions—almost exactly one-third of the outstanding amount of notes in the return given on p. 244. We thus arrive at the conclusion that, of the cash at the Bank of England which other banks use as the basis of credit, half may be taken as represented by securities and half by cash, and that this cash is itself represented as to one-third by securities and two-thirds by gold. The 20 millions of cash at the Bank of England are thus found to be based on £6,666,666 of actual gold.

And this is not all. For a considerable proportion of the cash in hand shown by the other banks will certainly consist of Bank of England notes, of which we have seen one-third to be represented by paper. Skill and success in the economy of metal could hardly be carried further.

The reasons which make a gold basis necessary for credit were traced in earlier chapters, and may be roughly summarized as arising from the fact that gold is the only commodity that is everywhere and always in the economically civilized world accepted in payment of a debt, and that readiness to meet liabilities in gold, at once and without question, is an essential part of a banker's business as understood in this country.

The liabilities of bankers to the public we have seen to be created, for the most part, by securities that they buy and advances that they make in one form or another, the advances being the much bigger item, and bankers' liabilities form the credits with which the financial and commercial body carries on its business, and against which it draws the cheques, which are the most important part of our currency. The problem of banking is the creation of these credits for the service of commerce, with due consideration for a sufficient basis of gold to meet the demands which these liabilities render possible A banker who holds too high a proportion of gold curtails his own or his shareholders' profits and the credit resources of the commercial community. The banker who holds too low a proportion runs a risk of being unable to meet his liabilities, to the detriment of his bank's credit, and with the possibility of raising a storm which might shake the whole banking community. Between these two evils the banker is asked to steer a middle course along the line of prudence and commonsense, and he is now convicted out of his own mouth of having erred a little on the side of making too much credit out of too little gold.

The fact that the banking world is in a position to air in public the existence of this error of its own is a comforting proof of its own confidence in itself, and indicates very clearly that the extent of the error is not considerable. It is the healthiest possible sign of the soundness of the banking position, and shows that the alarmists who point to the higher level of banking reserves held in other countries, and then draw terrifying inferences concerning the conditions prevalent here, are exciting themselves needlessly. As long as bankers are criticizing themselves and one another in public, we may be sure that the evil is not very deep-rooted. Nevertheless, the dangers involved by this evil, which have been pointed out above, are such that it should be removed at once. And so, though this book is only designed to make monetary matters a little clearer to those who do not understand them, it would not be complete without some account of the suggestions that have been made for the solution of the problem.

Among these suggestions many seem to indicate that the desired increase in the gold basis of credit is to be acquired by taking gold out of one pocket and putting it into the other. Whether it is to be done by the Treasury keeping a reserve against its banking liabilities to savings bank depositors, or by its repaying its debt to the Bank of England in gold, or by the establishment of a national gold reserve at the expense of the taxpayer, or by an issue of £1 notes against gold, or by the amassing of a special reserve by the banks to be deposited at the Bank of England under special safeguards, and only touched in times of need—and all these proposals have been put forward as a solution of the problem—it never seems to be observed that the amount of gold in the country will not be directly increased by any of them. For whether the Treasury or the bankers produced the gold for the new reserve or to repay the bank, etc., it could only be got by either taking it from the Bank of England's vaults and putting it back again, or by taking it out of the tills of the other banks and putting it into the Bank of

England's. And in either case the relation of the amount of credit to its gold base would be unaltered.

If, as is generally acknowledged in the City, the gold basis of our credit be inadequate, it must be increased—since we do not dig out gold in this country, and have no big hoards that can be drawn on in our stockings and our pockets—by imports, or rather by the retention of a larger proportion of the imports of gold which come here regularly week by week from the mines of Johannesburg.

These mines are the chief source which feeds the London bullion market. Every Saturday the Union Castle steamer from the Cape lands a parcel of raw gold from the Rand; every Monday it is dealt with in the bullion market, and after being refined goes to its purchaser. A certain proportion is always taken by "the trade," that is, the goldsmiths and others who use it in the arts and in commerce, and a certain proportion nearly always goes to India in the form of small and specially polished bars dear to native hoarders. The rest, if there be no competition, goes to the Bank of England, which pays for it, or gives credit for it, at the rate of £3 17*s.* 9*d.* per oz. When there is competition, foreign buyers take part of the parcel or all of it; and sometimes the Bank of England secures a share by paying rather more than its statutory price, though it rarely bids higher than 77*s.* 10½*d.*, which is the rate at which gold is coined into sovereigns. But gold is best secured or retained, not by bidding for it in the bullion market, but by influencing the foreign exchanges through the discount rate current in the open market.

It has been shown in preceding chapters that the foreign demand for gold chiefly depends on the state of the exchanges. If the Paris cheque is at 25*f.* 13*c.* it is cheaper for any one who has a remittance to make to France to send gold rather than buy a draft. And the state of the foreign exchanges is influenced by the market rate of discount; if the market rate is 1¼ per cent. here and 1¾ per cent. in Paris, French holders of English bills will not renew them as they fall due, but send them over to be collected and take the proceeds away; and, as we have seen that it pays better at a certain exchange to take the proceeds in gold than by the purchase of a draft, gold goes from London to Paris.

Sometimes the foreign demand for gold arises from uneasiness, financial or political, at some foreign centre, which impels it to bid eagerly for gold, even though it may not be the more profitable form of remittance. But these operations are abnormal and exceptional, and it may be said that as a general rule, and with allowance for the innumerable exceptions that complicate the working of the most watertight economic law, gold is taken from London when the exchanges are against us, and the exchanges are influenced by the market rate of discount, which affects the import and export of securities, and so the trade balance in the widest sense of the term.

It therefore seems to follow that in order to attract gold, or to retain a larger share of the gold that comes here from the English-owned mines in Johannesburg, it is necessary to have a temporarily higher level of discount rates here. For, if we set about the business in the only other possible way, by paying a higher price for gold than anybody else in the bullion market, it is most probable that we shall only make matters worse, because as fast as the gold is accumulated, the faster will discount rates go down, and the more the exchanges will go against us, and the keener will foreign competition for gold become. For as monetary matters are at present arranged, any increase in the gold reserve stimulates expectations of cheaper credit and encourages the bankers and bill-brokers to buy bills at lower rates.

Having thus groped our way to a conclusion as to the method by which an increase in the gold basis of credit is to be secured, let us try to discover who should bear the expense, if any, of the operations that have to be carried out. More gold is wanted, because it is considered by the banking community that the amount of currency and credit is too big for the foundation of gold on which it is based. The creation of this currency and credit is profitable to those who make them and to those who use them, in other words, to the bankers, including the Bank of England, and to the commercial and financial community, including the Government, which makes both permanent and occasional use of the credit machine. And it seems obviously fair that those who benefit by the extension and elasticity of our currency and credit system should make any sacrifice that may be necessary for the establishment of a stronger foundation for it.

When bankers approach this question they are fond of pointing an accusing finger at the Post-Office Savings Bank, and the fact that the Treasury keeps not one farthing of metallic reserve against the millions of liability that this bank has in its books; and they maintain that the Treasury ought to lead the way by making amends in this matter and providing a reserve of gold against the Savings Bank deposits. With all deference to the eminent authorities who have enunciated this theory, I venture to think that they are shooting at the wrong mark. The manner in which the Treasury has handled this question of Savings-Bank finance is open to vigorous and voluminous criticism, but it is happily irrelevant to the present problem. The Post-Office Savings Bank is not a bank in the ordinary sense of the word, and has nothing to do with this question of strengthening the basis of currency and credit, because it issues no currency and creates no credit. No one draws a cheque on the Post-Office Savings Bank, and no borrower goes to it with securities or bales of wool to ask it for an advance. It is a trust company rather than a bank, and the fact that it has the consolidated fund of the United Kingdom to draw on at need makes the provision of a gold reserve for it a needless and expensive luxury.

The point at which the Government touches on the gold reserve question lies rather in the fact that it is to a certain extent responsible for one of the weaknesses in the basis of credit and currency, by permitting the Bank of England to issue notes against a promise to pay by the Treasury. We have seen above that one of the assets held in the Bank's Issue Department against its note issue is a loan to the Government standing at eleven millions odd. Since the Bank Charter Act was passed the cheque has to a great extent taken the place of the note for the purpose of currency, and the note has become a basis of currency, being held chiefly by bankers in their tills and cash reserves, and as part of the foundation on which they build their fabric of credit. This being so, without any disrespect to the framers of the Act we can point out that a piece of paper which is used as a basis for currency and credit ought to be as little as possible based on other pieces of paper, in other words that the fiduciary part of the Bank's note issue might with advantage be reduced. And a very simple and obvious method of curtailing the proportion of paper that is behind the bank-note would be for the Government to repay gradually its book debt of eleven millions, perhaps at the rate of half a million or a million per annum, according to the prevalent conditions. There would be no need to ask the Treasury to make this repayment in gold and to expect it to go into the bullion market and bid for the necessary metal. I have tried to show that this is not the best way to increase the gold store, and in any case it is not an operation that the Treasury is well qualified to carry out. All that is wanted is that the Government should out of the Sinking Fund give the Bank a cheque for perhaps half a million a year, in redemption of its book debt, which heads the assets in the Issue Department. A small part of the Sinking Fund would be devoted to this purpose and would be redeeming debt, which is its business.

Let us see what would follow. In the Issue Department account in the Bank return the notes issued and the Government debt would both be reduced by half a million. In the Banking Department account the Public Deposits would be reduced by half a million and likewise the notes held on the other side, forming part of the Bank's reserve. The reduction in the Public Deposits would ultimately reduce the Other Deposits, because the use of Sinking Fund money for cancellation of this debt would reduce the amount that would otherwise be transferred to them through purchases of Consols or other stock. The proportion of metal behind the bank-note would thus be increased. If the process were sufficiently gradual it would cause no approach to monetary stringency; but it would insensibly narrow the paper basis of credit, and this narrowing would have to be made good by the attraction of gold to take the place of the cancelled paper. At the same time it is chiefly a waste of time to discuss such a measure, because in the first place it would imply an alteration in the Bank's charter and much Parliamentary discussion and delay; and in the second, since the profits of the Bank's fiduciary issue go to the Government, the loss following on its reduction would fall on the tax-payer, who would consequently look sourly on it. We must try some line of less resistance.

The attraction of gold to increase our store is best secured, as I have tried to show, by means of the market rate of discount. The market rate of discount is regulated in normal times chiefly by the action of the outer banks, and we thus arrive at their share in the operations which are necessary for the reinforcement of the basis of credit and currency.

Their share ought to be substantial. For they issue most of our modern currency in the form of cheque-books to be filled up by their customers, and manufacture most of the credit by making advances, discounting bills, and financing the discount houses. Any undue extension of credit that exists may fairly be laid at their door; for we have seen that the Bank of England, which is the greatest credit-maker of all, because the credits that it makes are regarded as cash by other credit-makers, exercises a self-denying restraint in the matter and habitually shows a very much higher proportion of cash to liabilities than the other banks.

Since, then, the other bankers are themselves responsible for the undue extension of credit, which they themselves have stated to be a problem requiring attention, it would seem that they themselves could very easily settle the matter, by quietly and gradually paring away the over-growth until the volume of credit was brought within a satisfactory relation to the cash on which it is based. And it would also seem that this simple process would be the more expeditiously set about because its operation, as we shall see, would itself have the effect of helping to attract or retain gold, so that the strengthening process would go on at both ends at once—the reduction of credit would increase the basis of credit, and the improvement in the proportion between the two would thus double its pace. Moreover, it would appear that a period of pronounced ease in the money market, due to slack trade and reaction after the American crisis, would be an ideal opportunity for the banks to set about curing the malady with which they find themselves to be afflicted.

This opportunity presented itself, and nothing was done. And for the very good reason that the banks are human. The need for reform has been put forward by big men in the banking world representing the big banks; and the lesser lights representing the smaller banks do not like the notion of seeming to be led or instructed. Moreover, it is, as a rule, the smaller banks that are the worst offenders in the matter of over-extension of credit, and they fear that a self-denying ordinance would affect their profits more than those of their bigger brethren. So they, or some of them, resent the whole discussion, urge that any restriction of credit would be bad for trade, refer the question to committees, ventilate proposals for the acquisition of gold by somebody else, and maintain that this is a national question which ought to be solved at the national expense, and so on. All this is very natural and reasonable and human, but does not quicken progress. And the advocates of reform are forced to the melancholy conclusion that agreement among the banks, which is the obvious and simple way of securing it, seems to be impossible.

This result is the more lamentable because the smaller banks are asked to do very little. Nobody suggests that a cast-iron rule ought to be laid down as to the proportion between cash and liabilities that a bank ought to keep. All that is needed is an extension of the publicity, which, partially and illogically applied, has already been coincident with a great increase in banking solidity and strength.

In other words, it is only suggested that the banks should show what proportion of cash to liabilities they habitually keep. This is already done by nearly all the biggest, strongest and most successful, and the adoption of the practice by the rest seems a most modest suggestion in the direction of reform.

We have seen in a former chapter that, under present arrangements, some banks publish a yearly balance-sheet, most of them a half-yearly, and a select few issue a monthly statement of cash and liabilities; of these last, one shows its average daily cash holding throughout the month, the rest show the position on one day. In the case of some of them it is known that this statement gives a fair view of their normal position, but in that of others it is suspected that loans are occasionally called in or bills are allowed to run off, with a view to making a good display of cash, so that the statement is to some extent misleading; and the habitual development towards stringency shown at the end of every month lends colour to this belief. The more acute development of stringency towards the end of each half-year, though to some extent due to other causes, also tends to show that the many banks which prepare balance-sheets only at those periods, restrict credits with the same object.

It is therefore contended that, if all banks regularly showed their habitual position, the over-extension of credit would at once be cured, because the over-extension of credit is carried out by the banks which do not issue periodical statements, or prepare for them by calling in loans. Therefore, say the advocates of reform, if all the banks agreed to make monthly statements showing their average position, not the position on a certain day, this calling in of loans when publicity is applied, and over-extension of loans when it is withdrawn, would be made impossible. Another suggestion with high authority behind it and probably equally efficacious, proposes that every bank should make a weekly statement.

It is pleasant to build castles in the air, even in the monetary air, and in spite of the difficulties in the way of this simple reform, let us see how it would work, and what effect it would have on this question of the gold reserve.

Its immediate effect would be the blotting out of a certain amount of credit which ought not to be in existence, because its makers themselves consider it advisable to blot it out temporarily, whenever they have to show their position. This effect would be inconvenient to the users of this credit, and so great care would have to be exercised, and the matter would have to be dealt with cautiously, gradually, and after due notice.

In consequence of this reduction of credit, loan rates would probably be temporarily higher and discount rates likewise. The trading community would find the process of financing itself rather more expensive, but need not be appreciably inconvenienced. The experience of the autumn of 1906 shows that trade can maintain great activity with a 6 per cent. Bank rate. It is highly important in the best interests of trade that banking credit should be soundly based, and the trader is obviously one of the parties who ought to be asked to contribute to any expense that may be involved by the improvement of its basis. The Government might, for a time, have to pay a higher rate on its Treasury bills, but the Government again, as a large and continuous user of credit, ought to contribute.

And though prophesying about economic processes is a dangerous amusement, there is every reason to expect that the higher level of rates established by the curtailment of credit would very quickly provide its own remedy by the attraction or retention of gold, and a consequent increase of the gold basis of credit resulting in its expansion to the old level. After that it would only be necessary to take care that the proper proportion is preserved, and this ought to be easily effected by means of the publicity which we are supposing ourselves to have secured, especially if at the same time a link, of the kind suggested in Chapter XII., could be established between Bank rate and market rate. Bank shareholders as a whole need suffer no loss; for a time there would be less bad credit made, but the price of good credit would be a shade higher, and this shade would probably suffice to maintain banking profits. Shareholders in banks which have never traded in bad credit would probably benefit, and the banks which have relied too much on the over-extension of credit for making profits would suffer some temporary loss, but ultimately benefit by being induced to reform their methods.

We have thus arrived at the conclusion that in order to improve the basis of credit it would be desirable, if it were possible, to reduce the amount of the Bank of England's fiduciary note issue by the gradual reduction of the Government's book debt to the Bank, thus making the bank-note, which is itself used as cash and a basis of credit, more a bullion certificate and less a credit instrument. But we dismissed this as impracticable, at present, owing to Parliamentary and political reasons and suggested—or repeated a suggestion that has high practical authority behind it—that much might be done if it were possible to curtail the supply of bad credit by inducing all the banks to show how much cash they habitually hold in proportion to their liabilities. And we showed some reason to believe that these measures would promptly increase the gold reserve, which is the metallic basis of credit, so enabling good and well-based credit to take the place of the bad and inflated credit that had been abolished.

As the gold came in attracted by the higher discount rate the balances of the other banks in the Bank of England would be increased; or if they preferred to increase their own cash holdings, they could take out bank-notes to hold in their tills, leaving the gold on which they were based in the vaults of the Bank of England. For it seems desirable that the strengthened gold reserve should be patent to the world, and it would be so more effectively if aggregated in the Bank of England than if scattered about in the vaults and tills of the other banks.

If once the apparently insuperable obstacles in the way of putting these measures into effect could be overcome, the process would work quickly, cheaply and effectively. And it need not be carried very far. England has no need to heap up a mountain of gold. Our banking system is happy in the possession of other reserves besides its metal, and with them we shall deal in the next chapter.

CHAPTER XV

OTHER RESERVES

It has been necessary to lay a good deal of stress on the necessity for an adequate proportion of gold among the assets held by bankers against the credits that they create for their customers, because in times of crisis gold is the only commodity that is of universal acceptance, because it is the essence of the English banking system that all demands are payable immediately in gold, and because a large holding of gold is thus the strongest evidence that a bank can show of its readiness to meet its engagements.

Nevertheless, it must not be inferred that a high proportion of gold is the only necessity, or is by itself sufficient for safety in banking. The national banks in certain cities of the United States are bound by law to keep a proportion of 25 per cent. of their deposits in gold or legal tenders, a higher proportion than any of our banks, except the Bank of England, think it necessary to show. And the United States has recently suffered from a panic in which its banks made no attempt to meet their liabilities, and their high proportion of cash did not save them from demands which they were quite unable to meet. It is no part of the task now attempted to trace the causes of this remarkable panic, but it was certainly not accounted for by lack of cash in the banks, though Mr. Mead's article in the *Atlantic Monthly* of February, 1908, already referred to,* has shown how the legal limit on the cash proportion of the national banks had been stultified by the growth of state banks which deposited part of their reserves with the national banks, so that a pyramid of banking credit had been built up on a cash reserve which had shown a steadily diminishing proportion to it

Lack of cash, though it did not cause the panic, thus appears to have been an important reason for the helplessness with which American banking succumbed before it. The more immediate influence which produced it, however, would seem to have been a conviction in the mind of the American public that the other assets held against the deposits of the United States banks had not been judiciously selected.

A dreary procession of scandals, disclosures, and revelations had shown that the methods of American finance had been in many ways questionable, and the suspicion had gone abroad that the banks had been too closely connected with these undesirable performances, and also that their

* Page 81.

investments and loans had been arranged to suit the convenience of groups of operators interested in Stock Exchange speculations. In the case of most of them the suspicion was probably groundless, but in banking matters the public does not easily discriminate, and the good banks and the bad fell under the same ban.

In England such a development as the control of a chain of banks by a gambling group, and the use of the banks' credit to further the group's gambling, is impossible. And the chief reason why we can bank with a comparatively small cash proportion, and with no legal obligation, is because English banking—in the expressive phrase of an American who recently discussed the matter with me—"works with a psychological reserve," that is to say, has won and keeps public confidence by means of the character of our bankers. It is because they are so sound, so straight, so sensible—from an American point of view, so unenterprising—that they are able to build a bigger credit fabric on a smaller gold basis, and even to carry this building to a height which they themselves have decided to be questionable. This psychological reserve is the priceless possession that has been handed down through generations of good bankers, and every individual of every generation that receives it can do something to maintain and improve it.

A high cash proportion is of little avail if the rest of the assets consist of securities which cannot readily be realized, of advances to insolvent customers against insufficient collateral, of bills of exchange drawn against anticipations of produce that may some day have a market, or of loans on real estate of great promise, but of problematical value if offered for immediate sale. The securities that a bank can hold among its assets are comparatively few; and the best of them, as has been frequently pointed out, are genuine bills of exchange representing real produce of universal demand moving into consumption.

Such bills pay themselves on maturity. The stocks dealt in on the Stock Exchange, which have to find a purchaser before they can be turned into cash, are thus in quite a different category, and it is only the best and most readily negotiable of them that can really be considered by a banker either as an investment or as collateral security for a loan. It need hardly be said that the fuller the extent to which securities meet the requirements of the austere banking ideal, the less the yield upon them will be, so that prudence and profits seem at first sight to point out different paths. And the possibility looks so extremely remote of any sudden application of the test of ready negotiability to banking assets, that the temptation to earn better profits by neglecting the dictates of the strictest prudence must often be almost irresistible. Whether they work for themselves or for shareholders, bankers are naturally impelled to try to earn good profits; a big dividend is so satisfactory an end to a half-year's work, and makes the shareholders' meeting so complacently complimentary and contented, that it must be difficult for bankers to remember that the strength of the bank is the first and last consideration, and the manner in which, on the whole, our bankers do so, is a remarkable exercise of patience.

They are doubtless fortified by the reflection that the extremely remote possibility of the application of the test of ready negotiability to banking assets is one of those occurrences which appear when least expected, and that the connection which international finance establishes between all the countries of the world makes an outbreak of mistrust anywhere else a cause of possible trouble everywhere, so that the area of possible disturbance has been enormously widened. It is all to the good that the American crisis of 1907 passed by without the smallest appearance of an inclination on the part of the English public to take money from the banks and hoard it, and it is pleasant to record that the Governor of the Bank of England, in a speech at an annual bankers' dinner delivered in July, 1908, paid a handsome compliment to the manner in which English bankers had met the crisis, and had carefully avoided the mistake that is sometimes committed by bankers in troublous times of calling in credits, and so creating an atmosphere of mistrust.

Nevertheless, now that that difficult corner has been successfully turned, and the business of credit-making goes on as if it had never existed, there can be no harm in pointing out that the danger was nearer and more real than was pleasant. An injudicious word in a newspaper might have sufficed to start the mischief, and it was within measurable distance of starting by itself. At least, a friend of mine—a solicitor of seasoned experience, and of a most unexcitable and unhysterical temperament—told me one Sunday morning in the course of the crisis that he did not at all like the look of things, and that he was thinking of withdrawing from his bank a large amount of clients' funds for which he was responsible. The chief influence which restrained him was the difficulty of knowing what to do with the money, and in what form to take it. The alternatives that suggested themselves to him were opening an account with the Bank of England, putting Bank of England notes away with a safe deposit company, or in his strong room at the Law Society, or burying gold in his back garden. While he doubted between these courses the financial sky cleared, and he finally did nothing. But if one man of strong common-sense and most conservative habit of mind was pondering these possibilities, it is more than probable that many others were doing likewise; and if the lessons of the American crisis are taken as meaning that English banking is so secure in the confidence of its home customers, that no infection of external trouble need be feared, bankers are laying a flattering unction to their souls. In fact, it demonstrated once more the perennial need for all the safeguards with which good banking can surround itself, adequate cash reserves, and careful selection of the rest of the assets held against deposits with a view to readiness of realization.

Another reserve possessed by English banking, which enables it to work with a smaller cash reserve than is considered necessary in other countries, is the fact that its gold is not locked up and protected by artificial means, but is immediately at the service of the first comer who presents a valid demand on it. It seems paradoxical that this unprotected state of the English gold store should enable us to do business safely with less of it, but it is literally true, because the practical result is that gold flows readily to London, when London signals for it with a high discount rate, since every one knows that gold which goes to London can be got back again. And the benefit that London confers on international banking, by providing this most useful facility of always obtaining gold, makes it most important for international banking to take care that London is not overstrained by performing this function. Because if these facilities that are given by London alone did not exist, the whole machinery of international banking would be thrown out of gear. Consequently, if a crisis became so severe that London had to restrict its facilities in this respect, other centres which habitually keep balances in London which they regard as equivalent to so much gold—because a draft on London is as good as gold—would find themselves very seriously inconvenienced. And it thus follows that it is to the interest of the other centres, which trade on these facilities which London alone gives, to take care that London's task is not made too difficult. This interest is especially strong in the case of the foreigners who keep a balance in London which is borrowed. London is continually lending its name on a bill, and giving credits, which make the cash of international transactions. In times of crisis it can cut down these credits, and call in loans from all the world. This power is in itself a reserve, but its exercise would take time, and the length of time would depend on the ability of our foreign debtors to get gold from their central banks. But the fact that foreigners habitually owe us large sums which we should call in if we were pressed makes them desire to save us from being pressed.

Hence comes the result that when a crisis arrives, as it did in the autumn of 1907, and an abnormal demand for gold in one country threatens to paralyze the international money market, the task of providing the required gold falls on London in the first place, but all other centres see that it is to their interest to give what help they can, and to relax some of the restraints and restrictions with which they protect their gold stores. In fact London drew in the gold required for New York from seventeen other countries. It must not be supposed that it did so entirely owing to the good-will and enlightened self-interest of those responsible for the currency arrangements of other centres. To a great extent the suction was compulsory, and arose from the determined use of the Bank rate pump by the Bank of England, and also from the fact that the United States were selling all that they could sell, and reducing their purchases to a minimum, and so compelling a stream of gold, through London, to themselves. But at the same time there can be no doubt that the readiness with which all the other countries produced coins and bars to send to London was greatly assisted by the knowledge that when all was over London would certainly send back their contributions as soon as they were in a position to ask for them.

Nevertheless, satisfactory as were the results

of the latest crisis in showing that London's power of drawing in gold is at least as strong as ever, it is not safe to base on them the inference that London can altogether neglect the question of its gold reserve and rely entirely on always being able to get gold in from other centres by raising its Bank rate.

In the first place, as has already been intimated, it is hard to be certain how much of the gold obtained in 1907 was brought by our Bank rate, and how much by the action of American finance, which called in its balances through London all over the world, and created new ones as fast as possible by selling everything that it could turn into cash.

In the second, it must be remembered that the crisis of 1907 was an American affair, and English banking was not affected by the smallest breath of suspicion. But if England had been the centre of disturbance, instead of the ministering angel, it is exceedingly doubtful whether gold would have come in as freely as it did. None of the other countries were willing to send gold to New York, which was the storm centre. London had to take the whole responsibility for doing that. And if London were itself the storm centre, who would there be to take its place and responsibilities? Imagination is struck dumb by the contemplation of what would happen if such a proposition were presented to the leaders of finance in other centres, and of the well-meant suggestions for international conferences and international clearing-house certificates which would be produced and ventilated as palliatives for a situation which would require prompt action, and the placing of a certain amount of gold in the place in which it is wanted.

Ultimately, and after delays that would be fatal, London could probably compel gold imports by sales of securities and commodities, and by calling in loans from foreign customers, but in the meantime the mischief that might be wrought is incalculable, and the mere suggestion of the possibilities of the position shows very clearly that London is a monetary physician who cannot afford, under any circumstances, to be sick. The confidence of its customers, both home and foreign, is an asset which enables the English banking system to provide an astonishing amount of credit on a very economical cash basis, but this confidence can only be maintained and secured by the strictest attention to the austerest rules of banking caution, expressed in a continuous strengthening of cash reserves, and increasing vigilance with regard to the soundness and negotiability of the other assets held against liabilities.

CHAPTER XVI

SUMMARY AND CONCLUSION

AFTER this long ramble through rough country, it is perhaps worth while to review and sum up the conclusions arrived at in its course.

We have seen that gold and silver were the commodities which universal acceptance advanced to the position of being taken in payment for all goods and services, and so became money as man emerged from the state of barter.

That gold finally reduced silver to a secondary place, and is now the only metal which is legal tender in England in payment of unlimited amounts, our silver coins being mere tokens, current by convention.

That banking economized the use of gold by the issue of bank-notes, payable on demand in gold by the issuing bank.

That, after a period of much groping and uncertainty concerning the principles which should regulate the note issue, the law laid down a hard-and-fast rule which stated the number of notes which might be issued in England against securities, ordaining that any more notes required by the commerce and finance of the country must be based on metal.

That this restriction of the basis of paper money was evaded by the banking community by means of the use of cheques, drawn against banking credit; that these cheques, though payable in gold on demand, are, to an overwhelming proportion, met by book entries, and crossed off against one another by the various banks through the mechanism of the Clearing house; and that their safety and convenience have almost ousted the bank-note and caused the cheque to take its place as the currency of commerce.

That the responsibility for the manufacture of currency and credit has thus passed into the hands of the banks, which carry it on without any restriction except that dictated by their own discretion and judgment.

That a credit system has thus been evolved of extraordinary elasticity and perfection, so perfect in fact that its perfection is its only weakness. This weakness arises from the ease with which credit and currency can be created without any relation to the gold basis on which they are ultimately founded, since gold is still the only form of payment that is certain of acceptance in times of crisis.

That this multiplication of credit increases the

difficulty of maintaining the gold reserve, a task which has been entrusted by custom and common consent to the Bank of England.

And though this book is intended merely as an elementary explanation, and not a criticism, still less an attempt at construction, we have amused ourselves by considering some of the many devices suggested by which the admitted inadequacy of the gold basis of our credit manufacture could be increased. And we came to the conclusion that the cheapest, simplest, and most efficacious would be (1) the establishment of a connection—quite elastic and only occasionally operative—between Bank rate and market rate, so that the power of the Bank to influence the foreign exchanges should not have to be enforced or created by artificial and clumsy methods; and (2) greater publicity of banking accounts, so that all banks should periodically show their position, not on any given day, but on the average throughout the preceding period. By this means it was hoped that much of the over-extension of credit now complained of would be abolished, and it might be possible to do away with the unfairness of the present system by which the strong prudent banks keep a strong prudent cash reserve, and their weaker brethren, sheltered behind their strength, carry on business in a manner which they are seemingly reluctant to submit to the test of publicity.

Measures of this kind could be carried out by bankers themselves, without any Parliamentary interference or discussion, which, once started, might lead to unforeseen and undesirable results. For this reason we dismissed as impracticable a reform which is theoretically attractive, namely, the reduction of Bank of England's fiduciary note issue.

It need not be supposed that the periodical statement of the average position is an unheard of and revolutionary principle, as applied to English banking. The Bank Act of 1844 provided "that a weekly account shall be sent by every banker issuing notes to the Commissioners of Stamps and Taxes, of the amount in circulation each day of the week; and also an average amount of the said weekly circulation; . . . the weekly average to be published in the *London Gazette*." Also "that the said Commissioners shall have full power to examine all books at all seasonable times, of such bankers as issue notes." These weekly averages appear to this day in the *London Gazette*, but the ousting of the bank-note by the cheque has robbed this effort by Parliament to secure publicity, of most of its intended effect.

We have seen how rough and heavy a hand this same Act laid on the delicate banking machine, prescribing that in future it was to issue no more notes except against metal, and so taking away from it all its power of economizing metal by the use of notes, and restricting its energies to printing bullion certificates. Happily the banking machine was able to evade these drastic restrictions, but the manner in which it was then handled should serve as a reminder to those who now manage it, that it is above all things desirable that they should themselves make some serious attempt to carry out the reform which has been pointed to as necessary by leading members of their own body.

INDEX

THE END

PRINTED BY WILLIAM CLOWES AND SONS, LIMITED, LONDON AND BECCLES.

Breinigsville, PA USA
06 March 2011
257015BV00003B/49/P
9 781163 404263